Before we begin…

It's a cliché to use the end of the year as an opportunity to reflect on where you've been, where you are and where you might go. Joyless philosophical types would have us believe that the calendar is merely a clumsy way to order our lives with no intrinsic existential or emotional meaning. Maybe so, but if there's two things we're not at It's Nice That it's joyless and philosophical.

So unapologetically we welcome the chance to celebrate the past 12 months and highlight in printed form some 150 projects which have engaged, inspired, impressed and excited us.

But before we launch headlong into our 2013 showcase of creative brilliance, allow us if you will a few words about what we've been up to →

This time last year It's Nice That had two websites; the main site and the Jobsboard. Sitting here today it feels incredible (in the most literal sense) to say that we now have seven (SEVEN!) as part of our network. We've launched our dedicated audio visual channel First Broadcast, our online shop Company of Parrots, our London listings site This At There, plus new sites for our annual creative symposium Here and our newly relaunched magazine Printed Pages (more of which anon).

This increase in offerings has allowed us to explore exciting new ways of our pursuing our top-line mission – to champion creativity across the art and design world. So whether that's a video series interviewing some of the people behind our favourite publications, bespoke T-Shirts commissioned from some of the best illustrators around or a new way of seeing at-a-glance how long you have to catch the capital's most interesting art and design exhibitions, we've embraced new opportunities in a way that kept our core values front and centre.

Our events arm too has enjoyed 12 months of exploring new formats and building on existing strengths. In December last year we returned to the Barbican for our second In Progress event, looking at the themes that had defined 2012 and how they might shape 2013 and beyond.

Unsurprisingly there was a decidedly Olympic bent and few memories stick out more than the torch designer Edward Barber handing one of his creations around the auditorium, or Channel 4's Dan Brooke speaking with humour and honesty about how the broadcaster approached the Paralympic Games coverage. But elsewhere speakers looked to the future, none more so than 3D printing expert Adrian Mars who predicted many of the legal and moral issues this cutting edge technology would go onto face with remarkable prescience.

Early in the 2013 we launched our shiny new events strand Nicer Tuesdays, an affordable, accessible monthly evening of talks that has taken in themes from creative mistakes to erotica, collaboration to London as inspiration with the likes of Rob Ryan, Antony Burrill and Sharmadean Reid. It's been a blast experimenting with this set-up and we're looking forward to where it will go over the next 12 months.

February also saw us take part in an intriguing search for what factors – both physical and psychological – made up the perfect creative environment.

Working with longtime friends of the site Represent, we ran the Ideal Studio project wherein we talked to 20 designers, studio managers, leadership experts, freelancers and architects about how best to strike that perfect balance of creativity and productivity.

Our own studio was thrown into excited turmoil on a Friday afternoon in March with the delivery of the first boxes of our relaunched magazine Printed Pages. We had deliberately given ourselves some time after the last issue of the It's Nice That magazine and thought long and hard about what we wanted to do in print and why we wanted to do it. From this long period of reflection and discussion we emerged with a clear vision of a magazine which was really accessible – through both its content and its price point – but whose visuals, design and tactile values would retain high priority. It sounded like maybe we were after the best of both worlds, but three issues in (and the fourth in the pipeline) we couldn't be more proud of what we have achieved.

It's hard to pick favourite moments from three magazines but where I think Printed Pages works best is when it tells stories that surprise, inform and entertain; we have never been interested in following the arts news cycle. So interviewing Stuart Smith about how he made the Tate Modern crack a reality, finding out about filmmaker Hanly Banks following Bill Callahan across America on tour and speaking to Guess Who? and My Little Pony illustrator Jon Goode all stand out as stories that maybe nobody else would have told. To all the writers, illustrators, photographers and interviewees who have been a part of it all, a huge and heartfelt thank you.

Another real highlight of the past 12 months have been the opportunities to engage with new creative audiences and facilitate new work in various ways. In April we were invited by the Tate Modern to host Off-Cuts, a two-day zine making workshop which took place as part of the gallery's annual Hyperlink festival. Teaming up with Zine Swap and designer Patrick Fry, we welcomed thousands of people over the weekend and helped them create their own zine re-imagining one of the Tate's famous works.

Also this year we set our first ever brief for D&AD, challenging students around the world to come up with new and exciting ways through which we could re-energise our relationship with the art school audience. The entries were spectacular both in terms of quality and quantity and after an intense day of judging we were thrilled to award Thomas Fitzmaurice a →

(i)

(ii)

(iii)

(iv)

(v)

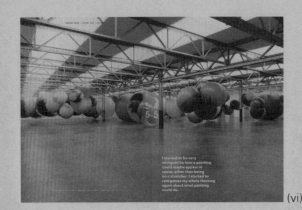

(vi)

(vii)

(viii)

(ix)

(x)

(xi)

coveted Yellow Pencil for his proposal to repurpose an ice cream van and tour universities with a mobile screen printing unit. As part of the link up with D&AD we also produced the magazine for this year's Student Awards, combining interviews with past winners and president Neville Brody with the winners across all 16 briefs.

This new way of engaging with young talent was combined with our long-running Graduates showcase. With more entries than ever before and the widest selection of universities represented in our final 12, the class of 2013 were a joy to discover and and an even bigger joy to meet face-to-face at the special Graduates event we held at the Red Bull Studios. Thanks again to Mike Radcliffe and his team at Represent for supporting this feature for the third year running.

As London's unusually gorgeous summer rolled around we were hard at work on our second Here symposium, held again in the sumptuous surroundings of the Royal Geographical Society. Some 600 delegates from across the creative industries were treated to an eclectic range of inspiring and insightful talks from a top-notch roster of speakers.

There were big names like Wayne Hemingway and Erik Kessels and younger talents like Nelly Ben Hayoun and Andy Rementer, flown in from as far afield as New York and Berlin, Barcelona, Amsterdam and Philadelphia. We heard how you organise a space orchestra, and the challenges of an installation full of rain where nobody gets wet; we found out how you design stage sets for Kanye West and witnessed a sexy song composed live on stage. But most importantly we got insights into these people's processes and discovered just how important it is to seize opportunities, to experiment, to fail and to turn conventional wisdom on its head. It was a magnificent celebration of creativity in all its weird and wonderful diversity.

If Here helped us bring some international talents to It's Nice That, we were also lucky enough to get away and visit terrific creatives around the world. This year we went north to Oslo, Copenhagen and Reykjavik, west to New York, east to Amsterdam, Berlin, Riga and the Milan Salone. We met great people, saw great work and spread the It's Nice That word as far and wide as possible.

Closer to home autumn brought with it the fantastic news that directors Will Hudson and Alex Bec had been made fellows of the London College of

Communications and we are looking forward to working closely with that institution over the coming year.

The studio filled up across the year and it is an honour to work with such passionate, dedicated and funny people every single day. But despite the last 1,465 words, this book isn't about us. Around 50 times every week we post on the site creative work that dazzles and delights us, in the hope and expectation that some of what we showcase sparks something in our readers.

But while naturally reaction to these articles is boiled down to the world of hits and visits, unique users and bounce rate, the response we get from people we feature can be measured in much more human terms. It's the illustrator emailing us after being commissioned by The New York Times or the artist taken on by a gallery the day after appearing on the site. It's the generous, humbling and excitable messages of thanks we receive on a daily basis. But the gratitude is all ours.

Naturally we couldn't fit everyone into these pages but without the insanely talented creatives whose work we are lucky enough to shout about to the world, none of this means anything (and we wouldn't all have jobs). So thanks to you, and in the unashamed spirit of end-of-year cliché, let's remind ourselves what a year it's been...

Rob Alderson, Editor-in-Chief

Colophon

Directors
Will Hudson and Alex Bec

Editor-in-Chief
Rob Alderson

Art Direction & Design
Commission
commissionstudio.com

Texts
Rob Alderson, James Cartwright, Liv Siddall and Maisie Skidmore

Illustrations
Jiro Bevis

Printed by
Park Communications

Thanks
Emily Beber, Ross Bryant, Anya Lawrence, Mike Radcliffe, Anna Trench and Holly Wilkins

To those who had faith in this annual from the start
Adam Kirby, Akshitha Victor, Alex Merto, Alex Simpkin, Alfred Dickson, Andrew Herzog, Anna Meier-Larsen, Arno Selvini, Benjamin Buysse, Benjamin Doughty, Bertrand Bruandet, Campbell Allan, Carley Ayres, Caroline Gilroy, Christine Cardus, Claire Doble, Conor Wynne, Costas Millas, Craig Jackson, Daniel Barrett, Daniel Maughan, Daniel Warrilow, David Payne, Diogo Lopes, Ellen Van Huffel, Erik Hoogendorp, Esme Heller, Eve Gray, Frank Baas, Gavin Mackie, Giorgio Chiappa, Henrietta Garside, Ian Braithwaite, Jack Gill, Jake Richardson, James Wynn-Higgins, Jérémie Martinez, Jo Briggs, Joao Carlos Costa Ribas D, Joe Addyman, Jonathan Barnett, Jonathan Davies, Jonathan Emmins, Jonathan Holden, Jordi Carles Subirà, Julian Roberts, Kara Harris, Kate Benjamin, Keeley Ashdown, Keith Woods, Kevin Farnham, Kyoto Studios, Laszlito Kovacs, Luke Roszkowski, Mandy Marxen, Mark Day, Matthew Box, Maureen Landy, Michael Bojkowski, Mikey Lland, Morgane Come, Paul Waddington, Thomas J Brightman, Nicholas Bec, Nicholas Maroussas, Paul Bean, Peter Allen, Peter Haynes, Peter Strauli, Philip Rodriguez, Richard Gray, Roy Killen, Ryan Berry, Sally Lewis, Sam Walker, Sean Clarke, Simon Brown, Simon Harrison, Sue Eves, Terry Clarke, Thankyou Thankyou Ltd, Thomas Fitzmaurice, Thomas Saunders, Tom Bentley, Vicki Munro, Wendy Cooper, William Hays.

Published by It's Nice That
11&13 Bateman's Row, London, EC2A 3HH

ISBN: 978-0-9564373-4-1

itsnicethat.com

It's Nice That →

ANNUAL 2013

"those luck
individuals
about v
creams an
nobody's b

y bronzed
wandering
vith ice
d lilos like
usiness…"

12

Andy Rementer

If you've followed It's Nice That for a while, then you're probably aware just how much we ruddy love Philadelphia-based illustrator Andy Rementer. The founder of the brilliant Techno Tuesday blog knocked our socks off afresh this year several times, but this work was the pick of the bunch. These bright, super-colourful images of life in Andy's version of New York – slightly skewed, volume up – are studies in human happenstance. Reminiscent of Edward Burra's work, this series cemented Andy's reputation as well as his place in our hearts.

7 Train from I Wish I Knew, Mondo Cane Gallery, New York

andyrementer.com

13
Nous Vous
& Studio Weave

Over the course of 12 months, certain themes emerge and lodge themselves in the collective creative consciousness, perpetuated by conference talks, articles and dissertations. Collaboration was certainly one of the hot topics of the past year, and no project we posted better demonstrates its potential than this amazing work, Ecology of Colour, by illustration collective Nous Vous and architects Studio Weave. Situated on Ecology Island in Central Park (no, the one in Dartford, Kent) this beautiful structure plays host to workshops and events designed to inspire the local community.

Photography: Jim Stephenson

nousvous.eu, studioweave.com

14

Patrick Leger

Forget the bogus rip-offs of Boy's Own annuals and odd, vintage style scouting books that can sometimes lurk in your Christmas stocking, Patrick Leger's drawings take all of that beautiful 1950s substance and aesthetic and combine it with sharp wit, ending up with truly spectacular drawings indeed. As well as being a favourite of commissioning editors at titles like Criterion, Esquire, The Times and heaps more, there probably isn't one drawing in Patrick's entire back catalogue that isn't fantastic, and that is why he's in the Annual.

Clockwise from top left: *Weeknotes* for Nokia/Gestalten Press; *Solutions For Being Stuck In An Unsatisfying Job* for Men's Health; *Networked* for Wired UK

patrick-leger.com

15 → 16, 17
Elisa Noguera Lopez

Last year's Annual featured several animal-based projects and it seems we're establishing something of a tradition with the inclusion of more pet-tastic photography. The poignantly-titled series Perhaps Finally Alone by Spanish photographer Elisa Noguera Lopez features a set of strange and surprising still-lifes – mainly animals' backsides – shot against backgrounds that range from the garish to the theatrical. Witty and unexpected, it's no great surprise that Elisa's work was one of the most viewed articles on It's Nice That in the past 12 months.

enl.cc

18, 19
Dan Wilton

Californian band The Bots have been described as "a cross between The White Stripes and Black Keys" and have garnered a lot of attention over the past year or so. Photographer Dan Wilton was lucky enough to go along for part of the ride, accompanying the duo on their European tour and documenting everything from intimate backstage moments to a trip to the world's largest pig museum. The photos positively crackle with exuberance and fun, and Dan went one step further, collecting his images into a really cool zine (which he packed with pig imagery in a further nice touch).

Clockwise from bottom left: *Boar Head, Schweine Museum; Anaiah's Arm; Anaiah, Online; Mikaiah; Tie Dye Shoe Session; Mikaiah, France; Mikaiah On The Road*

danwilton.co.uk

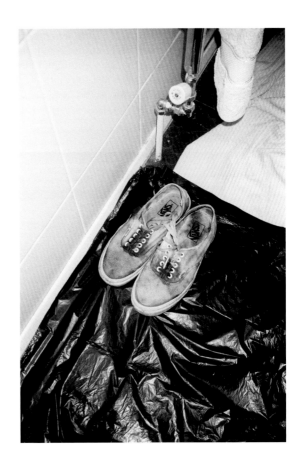

20

Fiona Ackerman

Versatility is one of the most impressive characteristics a creative talent can possess, and so Vancouver-based painter Fiona Ackerman blew our minds when we came across her work. While some of her work borders on the photoreal – scenes of scattered artist paraphernalia like paints and brushes – elsewhere Fiona's fabulous talent for visual storytelling emerges through pictures of walls of other pictures, or strange dioramas that compel and confuse in equal measure. There's an enjoyable sense that you're being toyed with – like a jocular uncle teases a favourite nephew – and that just adds to the fun.

The Calm Before The Storm

fionaackerman.com

21
Fons Hickmann m23

This is the first of two German opera projects whose graphic design we are going to laud in this Annual, but with good reason. Berlin studio Fons Hickmann m23 this year turned their prodigious talents to the catalogues for the Saxon State Opera's shows at Dresden's legendary Semperoper venue. The 2012/13 programme featured images of Dresden through the ages jostling for the eye's attention with vibrant blocks of colour, and they followed this up for the 2013/14 catalogue by splicing together imagery from around the world to create optical illusions. Simply great work from a studio at the top of its game.

fonshickmann.com

22, 23 ← 24
Kilian Eng

Ohhh Kilian Eng and your intense drawings of cavernous sci-fi cathedrals in distant lands. It's all very well drawing things from life, but can you honestly say that it's superior to the ability to invent entire other worlds? Kilian conjures up this kind of thing on the regular, making enormous, fascinatingly detailed pictures that are as emotionally stirring as they are meticulously drawn. The only drawback is that he's done almost too much good work, so going through it trying to find your favourite is a right ball-ache.

Previous page: *Palace Life IV;* Opposite: *Escape*

behance.net/kilianeng

25
M/M (Paris)

Even some design aficionados may look a bit blank if you mentioned Michaël Amzalag and Mathias Augustyniak, but namedrop M/M (Paris) and they'll know exactly who you're talking about. Since 1992 the French studio has blazed a trail of creative glory working across graphics, photography, films and interiors with galleries, fashion brands, magazines and musicians like Björk. This monograph – written by Emily King and designed by Graphic Thought Facility – combines insightful interviews with a whole host of jaw-dropping imagery. No wonder it's one of the most significant deign publications of the past 12 months.

Celebration Park for Pierre Huyghe Exhibtion; *Los Angeles* (top), A Film by Sarah Morris © Parallax. Both from *M to M of M/M (Paris)* by Emily King, published by Thames & Hudson

mmparis.com

HENRI CARTIER-BRESSON

words Jack Thurston

> *"Rather than document the action on the track, Cartier-Bresson sought to capture the deeper essence of the event, as revealed in the reactions of the spectators and the faces and bodies of the riders at rest"*

26

Rouleur

Cycling magazine Rouleur has been at the forefront of the independent publishing peloton for some time, but this year they made a break for glory with this extraordinary unseen work by Henri Cartier-Bresson. The legendary photographer shot this photo essay at the Vélodrome D'Hiver track in Paris in 1957, but they lay hidden in Magnum's archives until late 2012 when they were published in Rouleur 34. Amazing photographs by an amazing photographer and another reminder why great publications can still flourish – this was a shoe-in for the Annual 2013.

rouleur.cc

27

Dalton Maag

In last year's Annual we featured several projects inspired by or at least tangentially linked to the London Olympics, but this is the first work we've come across relating to the Rio de Janeiro Games set for 2016. Dalton Maag were commissioned by the organisers to create a bespoke typeface for use across all the Olympic collateral and they sought inspiration from Brazil's natural, architectural and cultural landmarks from the Christ The Redeemer statue to Samba football stars. What's really impressive about the font though is that it steers the perfect course between encapsulating something of the Brazilian spirit without feeling forced or stereotypical – roll on Rio 2016!

daltonmaag.com

28
Rob Pybus

There was a palpable thrill that ran through the It's Nice That editorial team when we first came across the work of Rob Pybus. The Brighton University graduate is a master at creating surreal, crowded scenes where the eye is drawn hither and thither in a relentless search for the next glorious aesthetic morsel. But while in some hands condensing this amount of life into an image could end up feeling uncomfortably crammed, Rob's bubblegum colour palette means his pictures just feel like being joyfully jostled by a passing carnival.

Boom Skates (Courtesy of Rob Pybus/ Agency Rush)

pybism.com

29
Daniel Kukla

Inspiration sometimes occurs just by looking at what's in front of you – for Brooklyn-based Daniel Kukla, that was his rearview mirror. Daniel was fascinated by documenting The Joshua Tree National Park where the Sonoran and the Mojave deserts meet in California, a paradoxically desolate place that is teeming with life. The photographer's plan came together after driving through the park and seeing the amazing vistas thrown up all around him, so he set about creating his own versions with the help of a huge plate glass mirror and his camera. The results – as you can see – are utterly spellbinding.

The Edge Effect: Hidden Valley

danielkukla.com

"unsure o

she'd l

to sit stil

amount o

f whether
e able
l for that
of time…"

2012

Alex Roulette

Alex Roulette's incredible surreal landscape paintings are executed with such a degree of research – from meticulously-sourced reference materials to careful environmental observation – they seem to be photographs of some idealised holiday or nostalgic moment from your past. The fictitious scenarios are entirely fragments of his imagination however, subtly harnessing Freud's ideas about the uncanny and our own curiosity about the strange displacement of one landscape into another. In this way they take you just beyond the border of your comfort zone to peek at the curious goings on on the other side.

Smoke Bomb

alexroulette.com

→ 33

Adrien Toubiana

Both red-blooded men and women will no doubt find Adrien Toubiana's images appealing, though we're certain it's not just a case of erotic attraction that makes them so good. There's a wonderful sense of narrative running through Adrien's photographs – a feeling of tension and suspense that culminates in a pleasingly obvious visual climax – but there's also mundanity there too (cereal and TV aren't exactly hallmarks of sexual intrigue). It's this casual eroticism that makes his images work so well, creating a free-love-era sense of benign sexuality that's all too rare in this day and age.

From Mon Petit Coeur Tombe en Panne Seche in collaboration with Eli Serres

adrientoubiana.com

Thomas Brown & Anna Burns

Do you enjoy watching ludicrously high-budget, high-octane, action blockbusters? Or are you more drawn to their low-grade counterparts, the B-movies where clunky dialogue and hammy acting joins forces with ridiculous explosions and two dimensional *femmes fatales*? Photographer Thomas Brown and set designer Anna Burns paid a unique kind of tribute to this cinematic genre in Pop Pop Bang , a series of installations where these movie motifs were printed on umbrellas and attached to huge scaffolding frames (some of which were then set on fire). A hybrid of household and Hollywood which was a bit weird, sure, but also pretty wonderful.

thomasbrown.info, annaburns.net

Detektiv Bureau

If we'd known as children that throwing paint around a plastic-covered room would have achieved such stunning results, we'd have been much messier kids. As it was our mums were pretty clear about where paint was and wasn't supposed to go so we never got the chance to make the kind of giant, beautiful installations that Swedish collective Detektiv Bureau produced during their month-long residency in Chicago last year. They covered everything in paint; from tables and chairs to the ceiling and floors. As immersive environments go, this is one of the finest we've seen.

detektivbureau.ch

37

Frederik Heyman

As far as we're concerned fashion is like a Pandora's Box of trouble which, once opened, can reveal all sorts of unpleasant surprises. Trying to keep up with what you should wear during what season is a minefield of which we'd prefer to stay well clear. That said, art director Frederik Heyman does a magnificent job of making the fashion world look surreal and exciting instead of just plain old intimidating, with incredible shoots for people like Kenzo and Vogue. They're so good that we were persuaded to take a much keener interest in the fashion world, and that's an achievement not to be sniffed at.

Honest By Muriée/Bruno Pieters campaign
Styling: Anne Pastré

frederikheyman.com

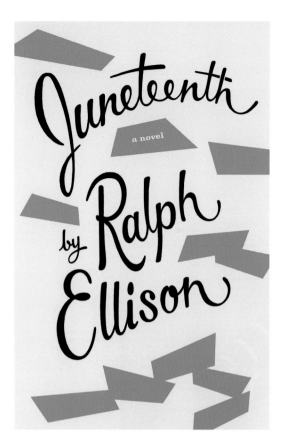

38

Cardon Webb

What Cardon Webb doesn't know about book jacket design isn't worth knowing. The New York-based designer has serious pedigree when it comes to creating lovingly crafted covers for some of the most groundbreaking literary figures of our time; from the complete works of Oliver Sacks to these jazz-inspired covers for the legendary Ralph Ellison. As a designer at Vintage Books, Cardon has plenty of opportunities to produce imagery for an enviable range of fiction, but even his work for lesser-known titles is charged with the same level of care and attention. Without doubt this is some of the best book design we've seen all year.

cardonwebb.com

Base Design

It's not often that large-scale arts organisations decide to embark on a complete brand overhaul; rarer still that they execute it without causing an outpouring of criticism. So for Base to successfully give the Haus der Kunst (one of Germany's foremost fine art institutions) a new visual identity with such little fuss was nothing short of miraculous. Really though it's not hard to see why the redesign was such a success. Based around a flexible logotype that affords numerous iterations depending on the requirements of each exhibition, Base have created an identity that always puts the artwork first letting the institution shine through the quality of work it exhibits.

Photography: Atelier KZG and Press Department © Haus der Kunst

basedesign.com

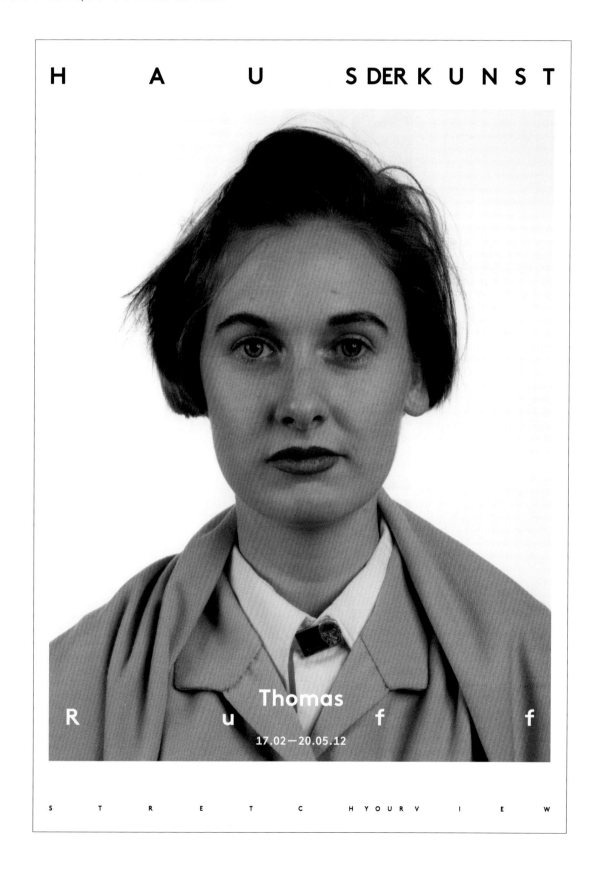

40

Craig & Karl

We've always been partial to a bit of Craig & Karl; an international illustration partnership who seem incapable of producing mediocre work. But we knew when they teamed up with Bureau Mirko Borsche, one of our favourite design studios, that the results of their partnership would be superb. Under Mirko's watchful eye the talented duo produced a beautiful selection of abstract forms for the Bayerishe Staatsoper's 2012-1013 season posters. The results are bright, bold and utterly gripping, adding a vibrant sense of fun and experimentation to the works of some seriously heavyweight classical composers.

craigandkarl.com

41

Bendik Kaltenborn

For our money Bendik Kaltenborn is as close as it gets to illustration perfection. Sure, it helps that he's produced album covers for Todd Terje (an artist who's seemingly always being played over the studio speakers) but his ability to add a sense of vibrancy to any subject he chooses is a truly admirable feat. Bendik's work has a timelessness that stems from his constant referencing of vintage illustration – the bright colours of the 1960s meeting spy thrillers of the 1950s – but the guys in his pictures clutch mobile phones, wear the latest fashions and are 100% from the here and now. It doesn't get much better than that.

benkalt.no

"I like to e

What keeps n

so in most ca

that crackin

you with a mu

and nut fragr

I deeply

t walnuts.

e from doing

ses is the fact

g a nut leaves

ltitude of shell

nents, a thing

bhor..."

2012

Lauren Francescone

I think we all know what's going on here. These lovely prints are cyanotypes, which is a process largely used by engineers when working with circles. Lauren's taken this starting point and run with it, culminating with this amazing series and securing her that rarest accolade; a place in our Annual two years in a row. She deserves great praise for managing to feature the trusty condom in her artwork without making it at all cringeworthy. Remember that kid you knew who did that angsty Art Foundation project where he made a statue out of contraceptive devices and then called it "Mummy"? Yeah, exactly.

Circles

laurenfrancescone.com

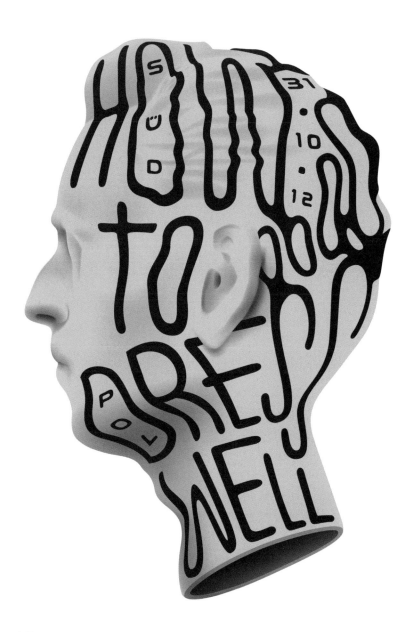

45

Feixen

Feixen is Felix Pfäffli, a Swiss graphic designer with many, many strings to his bow. He makes beautiful printed publications, arranges text with admirable skill, is a practiced editorial illustrator and we'll be damned if he doesn't make some of the best looking gig posters around. Felix has got it all; a great eye, enviable skill and exceptional taste in colour palettes. He also works collaboratively with his brother Mathis (also featured in this volume) making them the most talented sibling design duo we've ever encountered.

How To Dress Well for Suedpol, Switzerland

feixen.ch

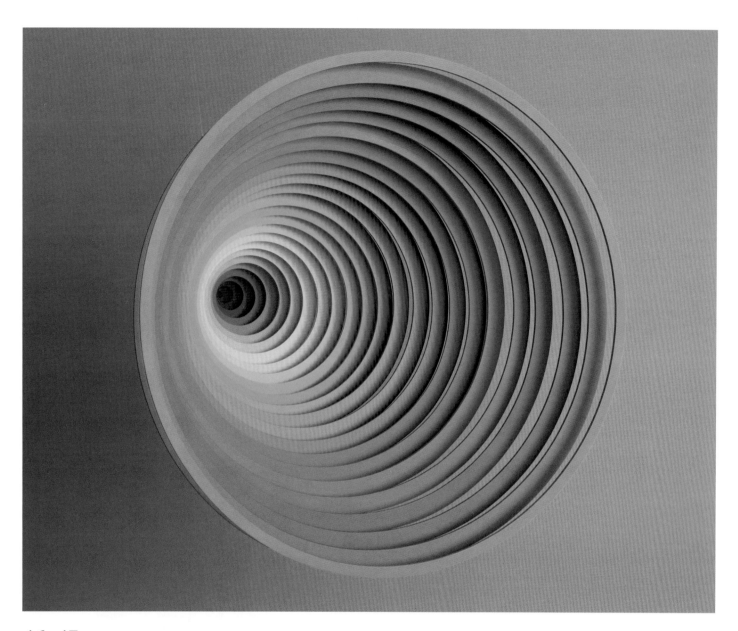

46, 47

Jen Stark

The idea of manipulation has pretty negative connotations, but with Jen Stark's work the viewer feels manipulated in the very best possible way. The Miami-born, Los Angeles based artist works across drawings, animation and painting but it's her sculptures which really stand out; stunning bright creations which combine shape, form, material and colour to create the most magnificently mindbending effects. With two big solo shows over the past 12 months (in her hometown and in Toronto) Jen's practice has assumed a confidence and poise which well suits one of the most exciting artists around.

Above: *Dimension*; Opposite: *Drippy*

jenstark.com

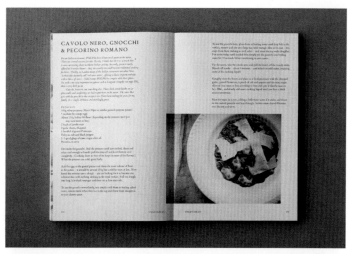

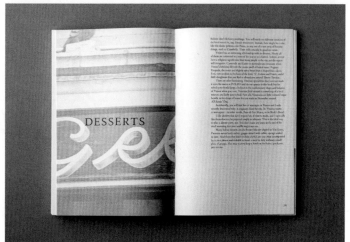

48
Praline

When it comes to creativity, awards are pretty spurious things – it's certainly not the case when we're putting this Annual together that we look back and try and to shoehorn in anything we featured on the site that went on to be garlanded. But in the case of Praline's beautiful cookbook for Russell Norman's Polpo, it was a happy coincidence that it was named Waterstone's Book Of The Year as it was already certain of its place within these pages. From the exposed spine to the Japanese stitching and the beautiful octopus illustration, this is printed matter that makes us purr.

From *POLPO a Venetian cookbook (of sorts)* by Russell Norman, published by Bloomsbury.

designbypraline.com

49

Simon John Thompson

How is it possible to describe Simon John Thompson's artwork? It's as if Walt Disney took acid and paid the entire animation crew from the 1950s to put together a storyboard for a violent, confusing film. You dig? Seriously, Simon's skills at making images like you've never seen before is unparalleled. Mix that with his extraordinary screen-printing abilities (that's five layers?!) and you've got yourself your new favourite illustrator. Like animals? Check out his brand new series of animal portraits, then email the man and buy one for above your fireplace, stat!

Wolf

simon-john-thompson.com

50
Studio Large

We're not entirely sure how Belgium-based Studio Large got its name. It could refer to the range of work they produce or the amount of talent these four prodigious designers boast between them. What's certain is that when Bureau Mirko Borsche are coming to you for experimental typography then you're skills are very well-respected, but beyond fonts these guys have art directed interesting publications and created excellent digital illustrations. We'll be keeping a close eye on this studio next year and beyond.

Suspense for Faites Vos Jeux at Le Syndicat Potentiel in Strasbourg

large.la

You can't get any closer to the news.

Cape Times

England's fearless leader

Know all about it.

51

Lowe Cape Town

If the new millennium saw social media begin its unstoppable rise to scarily dominant cultural force, then 2013 is definitely the year in which the selfie well and truly came into its own. At times it seemed nigh on impossible to step out into the street without coming across a teenager, wannabe model or couple pouting furiously at their own reflection in a shiny screen. Lowe Cape Town harnessed this new social phenomenon to hilarious results with their Cam Whoring campaign for the Cape Times newspaper, in which they manipulated iconic and historical images to make the subjects seem to be taking pictures of themselves. This combined clever advertising, unashamed narcissism and tongue-in-cheek humour at their very best.

aloweprofile.co.za

Mark Leary

If you're a cycling enthusiast who enjoys the odd rainbow, stop what you're doing and have a look at the photography of Mark Leary. Scenery hasn't looked this psychedelic since the LSD-fuelled 1960s, and this is all down to his unique method of using two Ebony field cameras that function using plates instead of ordinary film. Of all the sporting photography we've seen this year - and there's been a lot - nothing has proved to be quite as beautiful and unique as Mark's stunning images of the Tour de France.

Previous page: *Norwegian Flag*

mark-leary.com

54, 55

Brendan Monroe

We have got a seriously soft spot for Brendan's artwork. Every now and again, when the moon is full, a publication will plop delicately into the office and it will be one of Brendan's quiet, unassuming tales of love, time, evolution and friendship. Saying that, the content's only part of the perfect package alongside the meticulously printed book that it's housed in. Islands n.2 is a strange little tale of two lovers, a midnight beach and the birth of the world. It honestly feels like the whole publication is drawn, printed and bound with ink and paper laced with love.

brendanmonroe.tumblr.com

56, 57
Vincent Fournier

If you've been taking monotonous photos of your meals and friends' dogs and calling yourself a photographer, then look away now. No, wait, don't look away – look at Vincent Fournier and take note. Among his numerous mind-blowing projects, Vincent has amassed a series focussing on a whole range of intergalactically-obsessed people and places. From astronauts to astrophysicists and space stations to classrooms, Vincent captures the real nature of this world which is so often steeped in wonder and awe.

Ergol #2, Final Assembly Building [BAF] 65, Arianespace, Guiana Space Center [CGS], Kourou

vincentfournier.co.uk

"a faded palette you'll to eat

colour
so good
want
it..."

2013

60
Heidi Voet

Celebrity gossip magazines enjoy nothing more than likening women's bodies to various fruit and vegetables, leaving women to choose between the unfortunate pear-shape and the much-coveted butternut squash. So Heidi Voet's photographic series Fruit & Vegetables, which visually completes women's bodies with foods most commonly found on a greengrocer's stand, got a hearty giggle from us. The concept which underpins the images is no joke though; Heidi's pairings highlight the consumption and limited preservability of both parties, as well as the reduction of women to the sum of their parts, so her brilliant idea gently probes established notions of physicality in a fun yet thought-provoking way.

heidivoet.net

Sam Vanallemeersch

When we first wrote about Sam Vanallemeersch we expressed feelings of envy, inadequacy and intense admiration for this most impressive of artistic talents. In time we hoped these feelings would diminish, but as the days march on we find them only increasing in strength. Sam is the complete illustrator, channeling every inch of his being into his work and communicating with incredible narrative complexity and compositional skill – man this guy can draw! Unlike most of his peers Sam isn't afraid to work with different visual languages either, honing two different styles of work to a level of polish that most couldn't achieve with one. Mind-blowingly good on so many different levels.

Below: *Lydia Davis;* Next page: *Rain*

sovchoz.be

Sam Vanallemeersch

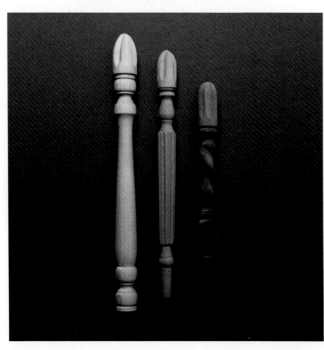

64, 65
Loris & Livia

There are, unfortunately, fewer and fewer outlets for brilliant craftsmanship in today's increasingly digital creative sphere, so when we stumble across a practitioner (or pair of practitioners) who know how to make truly beautiful objects with classic, timeless methods we tend to grab them with both hands and shout about them from the rooftops. This is where Loris and Livia come in; their Lemon Toys projects is a reformation of stair balusters into traditional wooden lemon reamers. Each unique piece is hard-carved from beech, mahogany, ash or English oak, and the final result is something you'd be proud to have in your kitchen.

lorisetlivia.com

66

Arjan Benning

Going above and beyond the weird and unexpected are those images which fill the viewer with the sensation that something is amiss, without letting on exactly what that might be. Arjan Benning fits this brief perfectly with his photographs of curious sequences of events; from inanimate technological objects which have been sawn in half, to colours and surfaces so rich that they take on a kind of visceral, flesh-like nature, skirting the border, as he explains, "where authenticity and amazement are close together." We were blown away by the combination of textures in his dreamy wonderland and we're still drawn to them all these months later.

Above: *Untitled,* Styling: Mirella Sahetapi;
Below: *Untitled* Styling: Judith Rasenberg

arjanbenning.com

Simon Hanselmann

We have nothing but nostalgic childhood recollections of Helen Nicoll's Meg and Mog stories, illustrated by Jan Pienkowski, so Tasmanian Simon Hanselmann's brilliantly twisted 21st Century variation on the original was a welcome defilement of our memories. Between the extra "g"s, Megg's new green tinge, the "sadness mattress" and the ongoing theme of methadone addiction, Simon's stoner reinterpretation of the classic comic had us absolutely enthralled, proving the adage that if you can't beat the original, drag it somewhere dark and disturbing instead.

From Bad Brains for Space Face Books

girlmountain.tumblr.com

68, 69 ← 70
Hondelatte-Laporte

It takes the very best kind of architect to find a way of injecting a dose of pure, unadulterated joy into your daily surroundings, and Raphaëlle Hondelatte and Mathieu Laporte have seemingly made this their aim. The appropriately-named Giraffe Children's Centre in Paris features a huge yellow giraffe whose legs you have to walk through to reach the front door, and whose head peers watchfully over the building. As Hondelatte-Laporte explain: "Architecture turns into storytelling. The building changes its identity and becomes a landscape in its own right, a metaphor for the urban jungle."

Photography: P.Ruault

hondelatte-laporte.com

71

Eiko Ojala

Estonia's art and design scene may be distinctly underrepresented on It's Nice That, but the brilliant illustrator, graphic designer and art director Eiko Ojala is doing an admirable job of shouldering the burden for his country. Eiko swept us off our feet with his innovative paper collages, which he applies to great effect across an incredibly broad spectrum of design projects. Creating detail using perforation, folding and layering techniques, Eiko's skill with paper and scissors surpasses that of any designer we've seen this year.

Professor

ploom.tv

72, 73
Merijn Hos

Merijn Hos is a Dutch illustrator with a larger back-catalogue than the Argos index. We fell in love with his image-making some time ago but were wowed anew this year. Merijn put on an extraordinary show at the Beginnings gallery in New York, filling the space with nearly 300 small, wooden figurines, hand-painted by the man himself. From birds, to girls, to bears, to mythical creatures, the characters created on these little statuettes are so funny and full of personality that you can almost guarantee they talk to each other after lights out.

Wood Sculptures

merijnhos.com

CHRIS COHEN Monday 3 June / The Victoria /451 Queensbridge Road Dalston, E8 3AS / 8:00 | £7
Presented by Upset the rhythm / poster art: sergiomembrillas.com

74

Sergio Membrillas

Sergio Membrillas is one of a bunch of brilliant illustrators who managed to scoop the classic gig poster from the clutches of the gaping black hole it was seemingly set to tumble into this year, quickly resuscitating it with no small dose of pizzazz. His particular brand of poster design blends retro and contemporary styles together seamlessly with his muted palette, fancy fonts and a whole series of thoroughly charming characters, to create an enduring identity for the bands he represents.

Chris Cohen for Upset The Rhythm

sergiomembrillas.com

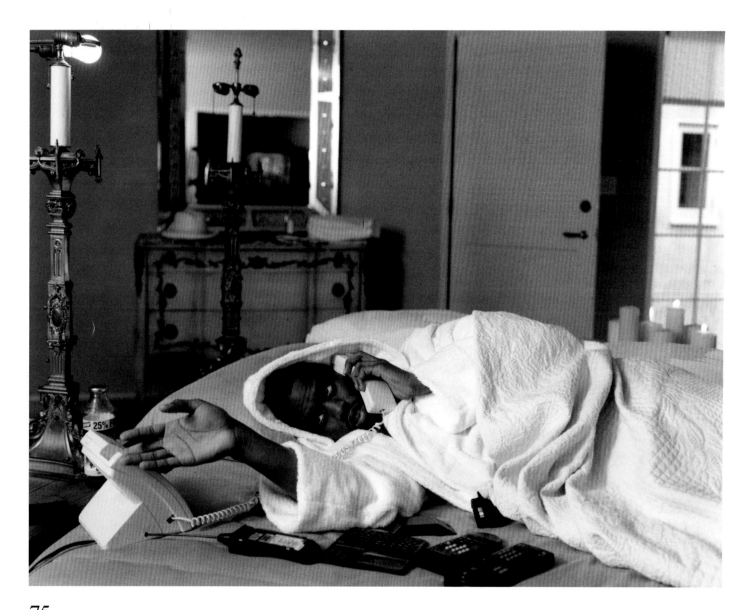

75

Dana Lixenberg

The sheer breadth of subject matter photographer Dana Lixenberg's lens reaches is truly astounding. Her personal projects tend to focus on individuals and communities living on the margins of society; we were most beguiled by her portraits though. From Bob Guccione to Gael García Bernal and Susan Sontag to P Diddy, she succeeds time and again in capturing the essence of her subjects, in all of their nuance and diversity, while still creating images which are stand-alone works of art.

Puff Daddy

danalixenberg.com

76
Studio Newwork

Design is an industry that respects few boundaries; disciplinary, generational or international. This latter truth was proved this year by New York-based Studio Newwork's identity for a German cultural festival held in Japan. Deutschlandfest takes place in Tokyo and Newwork approached with a paradoxical blend of strong ideas and restraint. Influenced by Japanese kanji characters, the yellow, black and red of the German flag and the Bauhaus, they crated a smart and communicative look which worked across various visual collateral. As cross-cultural mash-ups go, few were as successful as this in the past 12 months.

studionewwork.com

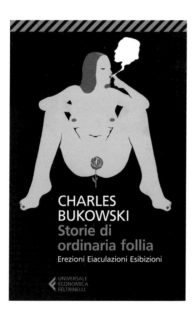

77

Emiliano Ponzi

As Charles Bukowski fans and critics alike will happily tell you, his novels reek with a potent mixture of testosterone and decay, along with a little nihilistic displeasure. So how exactly does one go about designing a cover for books by a writer once labelled the "laureate of American lowlife"? Emiliano Ponzi seems to be the man to ask; his designs for Italian publisher Feltrinelli's Bukowski series won a gold medal at the Society of Illustrators in New York, and they impressed the pants off us too. They combine the books' themes with the charisma of the author who penned them, capturing exactly Bukowski's salacious allure.

emilianoponzi.com

The Shov

vs That...

The show that brought us a creative at the top of his game.
Juergen Teller, Woo! **at the ICA London.**

January 23 until March 17 2013
Photography: Mark Blowe

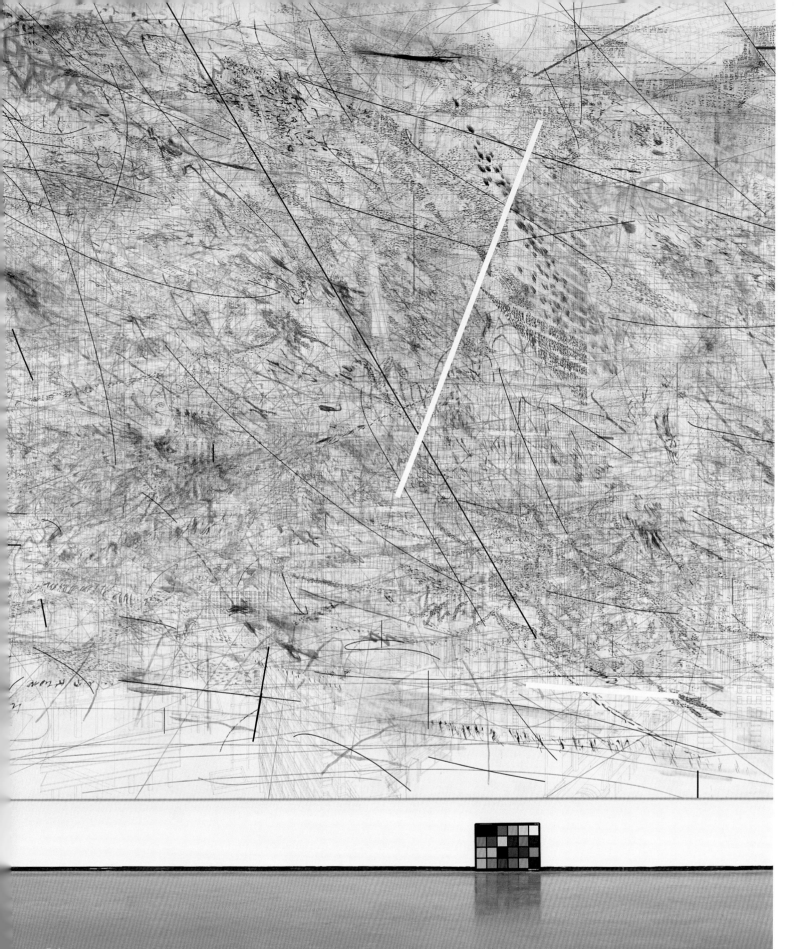

The show that scrambled ideas of urban space. *Julie Mehretu,*
Liminal Squared **at White Cube Bermondsey, London.**

May 1 until July 7 2013
Photography: Ben Westoby

82
The show that made dreamscapes out of tapestries.
Kustaa Saksi, Hypnopompic **at Korjaamo Gellery, Helsinki.**
August 16 until September 15 2013

The show that let us all play at being Spiderman. *Leandro Erlich*, *Dalston House* at Ashwin Street space with The Barbican, London.

June 26 until August 4 2013
Photography: Gar Powell-Evans

The show that razzle-dazzled our retinas. *Light Show* at **Hayward Gallery, London.**

January 30 until May 6 2013
Photography: Linda Nylind

85

The show that turned simple thread into something astonishing.
Pae White, Too Much Night, Again at South London Gallery, London.

June 26 until August 4 2013
Photography: Andy Keate

The show that let us wrongfoot the rain. *rAndom International,*
Rain Room at The Barbican, London.

October 4 2012 until March 3 2013
Photography: Felix Clay

The show that brightened up our summer *Ryan Todd*
at Kemistry Gallery, London.

June 6 until June 29 2013

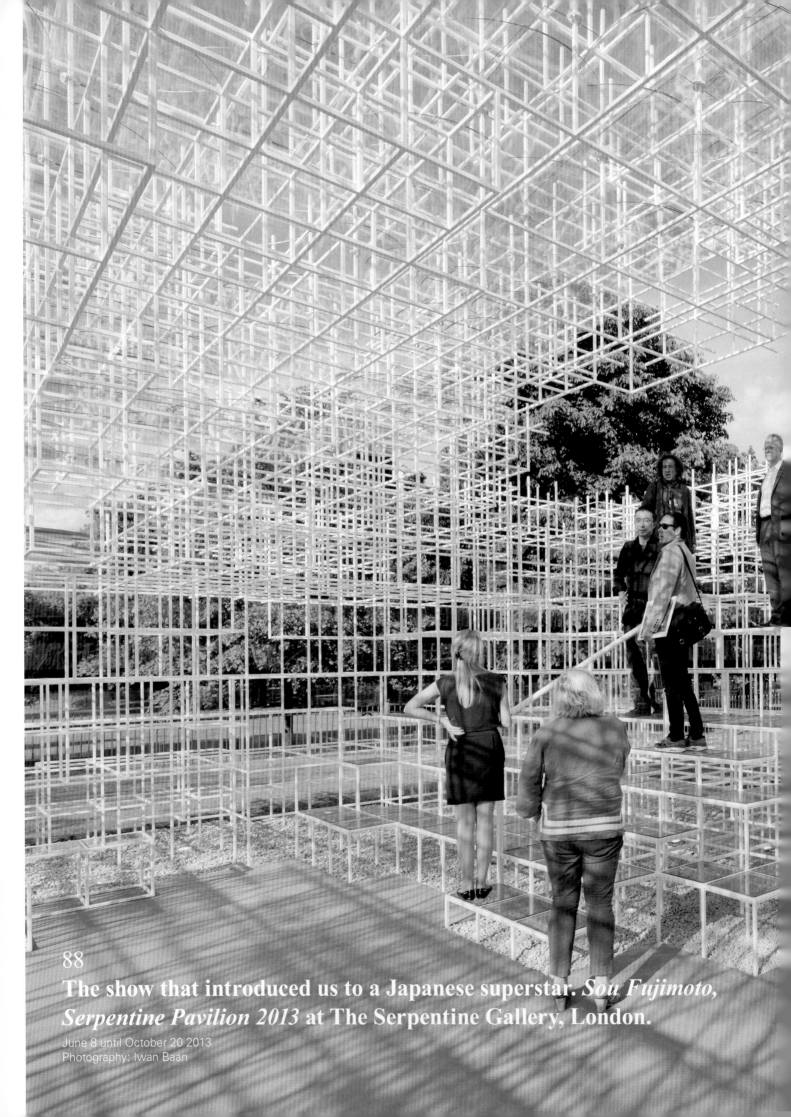

The show that introduced us to a Japanese superstar. *Sou Fujimoto,*
Serpentine Pavilion 2013 at The Serpentine Gallery, London.

June 8 until October 20 2013
Photography: Iwan Baan

89
The show with the most terrifying giant props. *Tim Walker,*
Storyteller **at Somerset House, London.**

October 18 until January 27 2013
Photography: James Stopforth

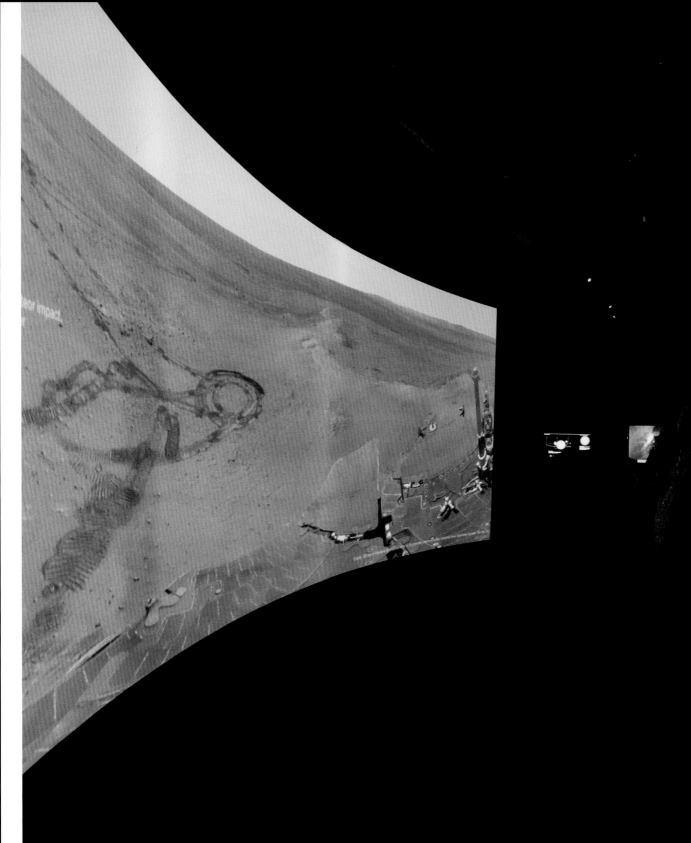

The show that blew our tiny minds, space style. *Visions of the Un* at the National Maritime Museum, London.

June 7 until September 15 2013

91

The show that had the best title of the year. *Why Not Associates,*
We Never Had A Plan So Nothing Could Go Wrong **at Ginza Graphic**
Gallery, Tokyo.

June 5 until June 29 2013

"giant
multi-c
pvc

orbs of
oloured

,,
...

2013

94

Alejandro Almanza Pereda

There's something illicitly thrilling about looking at something so precarious it may come crashing down at any moment, a deliciously shameful anticipatory sense that gets the heart pounding. This is perfectly demonstrated by Mexican artist Alejandro Almanza Pereda who's now based in New York and creates mindbending sculptures which combine furniture, glasses, bowling balls and lights to insane effect, all seemingly on the verge of imminent collapse. This piece also includes "a Qing dynasty Chinese bronze libation vessel, a Nigerian Yoruba brass equestrian figure and a 1927 stone from the College of Wooster Memorial Chapel." So yeah, this is art the likes of which we don't come across every day.

Spare The Rod And Spoil The Child

alejandroalmanzapereda.com

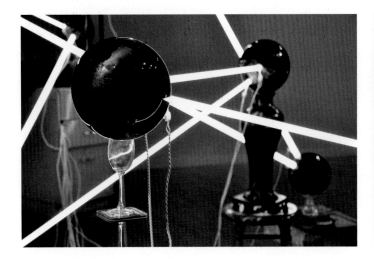

95
Bryan Olson

Now no one's saying that Bryan Olson is the first man to make cool collages out of cool pictures from the olden days; we get that it's been done before. It's just that Bryan is really, really good at doing it. He can transform a European market scene into a sci-fi film in one step. He can turn green farms into the pastures of the afterlife, he can make a hole in the sky and poke a book through it. It's not about how good his images are (they're mighty fine by the way) it's more about the stories he's inspiring in your mind. You dig?

Ultrastructures

bryanolsoncollage.com

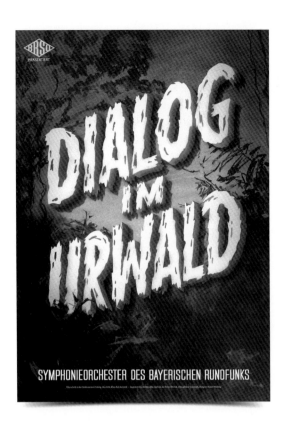

96, 97
Bureau Mirko Borsche

Another German design studio, another project for a classical music institution but you know what, we make no apologies for that. These posters for the Symphonieorchester des Bayerischen Rundfunks illustrated by Beni Haslimeier reimagine the sometimes slightly stuffy world as a series of 1940s inspired posters, full of the typographic touches and communicative excitement of the golden age of the silver screen. It's a simple idea for sure but anything less than perfect execution would bring the whole thing crashing down. As it is the power of the poster is proved once again.

mirkoborsche.com

THE FUNKY RUNDFUNKS WOW CARNEGIE HALL

SYMPHONIEORCHESTER DES BAYERISCHEN RUNDFUNKS

das Leben in den Seufzern

SYMPHONIEORCHESTER DES BAYERISCHEN RUNDFUNKS

DER KERN

SYMPHONIEORCHESTER DES BAYERISCHEN RUNDFUNKS

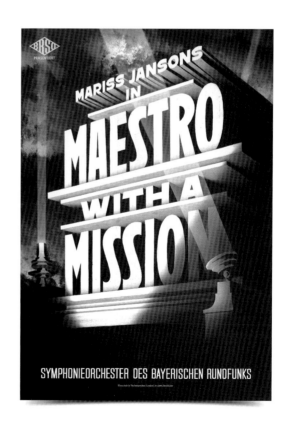

MARISS JANSONS IN MAESTRO WITH A MISSION

SYMPHONIEORCHESTER DES BAYERISCHEN RUNDFUNKS

98, 99

Jean Jullien

The ongoing anxiety about our relationship with modern technology is an issue that has exercised philosophers, writers, academics and creatives of every stripe. But few have addressed this topic – which in the wrong hands has the potential to be clunkily obvious – better than illustrator Jean Jullien. His brilliant take on the sheer inhumanity of our dependence on the latest gadgets is second to none as he renders the way we increasingly subjugate experiences – be it live music, communing with nature or with each other – to the capture-and-publish world of social media. Another stellar step in Jean's meteoric rise.

Allo; I Feel So Online

jeanjullien.com

100
Jim'll Paint It

We like to think we know a sure-fire pop culture phenomenon when we come across one and this was certainly true of the brilliantly absurd Jim'll Paint It blog. The idea is simplicity itself – Jim invites readers to suggest scenes they would like to see and he duly creates them using retro artistic tool par excellence Microsoft Paint. The requests are almost uniformly hilarious and preposterous, often involving a mixture of celebrities (think Moby, Hulk Hogan or Ross Kemp) bizarre scenarios and amazingly specific twists which Jim heroically renders in minute detail. Silly, sure, but oh so worth it.

A Tyrannosaurus Rex playing Connect 4 with Heston Blumenthal on a lake of fire whilst a Care Bear watches them lustfully. Suggested by iknockthingsover and © Like Regular Chickens Ltd

jimllpaintit.tumblr.com

101

Juno Calypso

First things first, nobody in this entire Annual has a cooler name than Juno Calypso, but this recent graduate of the London College of Communications is so much more than a snazzy moniker. Under the guise of alter ego Joyce, Juno photographs herself in an array of scenarios (bursting out of a cake say, or sprawled on her dressing gown on a bed) which become really unsettling due to the garish composition and strange expressions she assumes. Her work seems to reference the vacuity of celebrity culture and the pressure to conform to certain societal expectations but these are hints and whispers, deliberately obfuscated by this singular talent.

A Modern Hallucination

junocalypso.com

102, 103
John Schabel

There's been a lot of discussion this year around photography projects with unsuspecting subjects, ignited by Arne Svenson's The Neighbours series for which he was taken to court. We're not sure whether John Schabel's images have landed him in any hot water and to be honest we hope they haven't because they're brilliant. Back in the 1990s, John waited with his camera next to airport runways and photographed airline passengers as their planes passed him by – the resulting images (published this year) are haunting, poignant snapshots of people in private contemplative moments.

Passengers (Courtesy of Twin Palms Publishers)

westcollection.org/index.php/artist/index/793

104, 105

Jonas Unger

Amid the visual cacophony of images we are exposed to every year, one or two for some reason manage to lodge themselves in our imagination and come to define that particular period of time. So it was with Jonas Unger's photographs of eccentric actor Gérard Depardieu for Die Zeit Magazin, or to be more precise the image of Gérard bombing through the Loire Valley countryside on a moped. Jonas' portfolio proves this shoot was no fluke; time and again his daring approach and eye for composition confirm him as one of the most exciting portrait photographers around.

Pope Benedict; Gérard Depardieu

jonasunger.com

106

Zigmunds Lapsa

It's Nice That prides itself on the international scope of its art and design coverage and so it's a double pleasure to see Latvian graphic designer Zigmunds Lapsa showcased in this Annual. Riga has a small but incredibly passionate design community working on a whole host of interesting projects and Zigmunds is one of its foremost practitioners (although just as we went to press we heard he has now moved to London). Whether turning his talents to book covers, posters, magazines or environmental design, Zigmunds combines excellent ideas, a surefooted palette and an ability to marshall both graphic and illustrated elements with real flair.

Dizaina Studija cover

zigmundslapsa.com

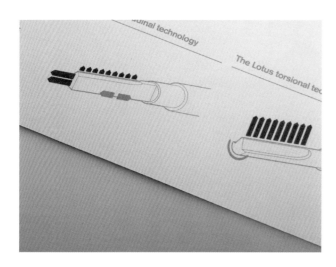

107

Mytton Williams

And the award for the most unexpectedly great graphic design of the past 12 months almost certainly goes to Mytton Williams' identity and packaging for the Lotus ultrasonic scalpel. The Bath-based studio oversaw everything from the typography to the striped coloured packaging and – most crucially of all to be honest – the explanatory inserts that walk surgeons through how this equipment works. It's proof not only of Mytton Williams' considerable talents but also that really excellent design treatments don't begin and end with posters and book jackets, as the blogosphere might sometimes have us believe.

myttonwilliams.co.uk

"the boys from
erotically ag
panelled back
Welch curtsy
poolside and S
Lion) looking p
in a darker

Seetal Solanki

Justice staring against a wood-drop, Florence ing by an LA oop Dogg (now ositively tearful ed room…"

A2/SW/HK

Publication redesigns are rarely an easy undertaking and the pitfalls of overhauling a well-loved periodical are often enough to put off even the most hardened art director. When the publication's as well-respected and genre-defining as photography title Aperture the stakes are that much higher and the risk of incurring the wrath of an army of loyal readers enormously pressing. Thankfully the Aperture team worked with A2/SW/HK on the project, a studio famed for its editorial pedigree and typographic rigour. The results are exemplary and breathe new life into a magazine that's always strived for greatness. As far as we're aware, no subscribers were lost in the process.

a2swhk.co.uk

113
Comet Substance

We see a lot of posters on our daily hunt for great creative work; more than you can feasibly imagine in fact. As a result when we come across something that stands out instantaneously for its originality, we jump at the chance to write about it. Ronny Hunger, or Comet Substance as he's aliased himself, makes posters that are absolutely original; small runs of screen prints for music venues in his native Switzerland that bring together found photography, hand-drawn elements and vintage type, hinting at the variety of creative influences that inspire the bands they promote.

Mt. Vine (Artist: Ronny Hunger)

cometsubstance.com

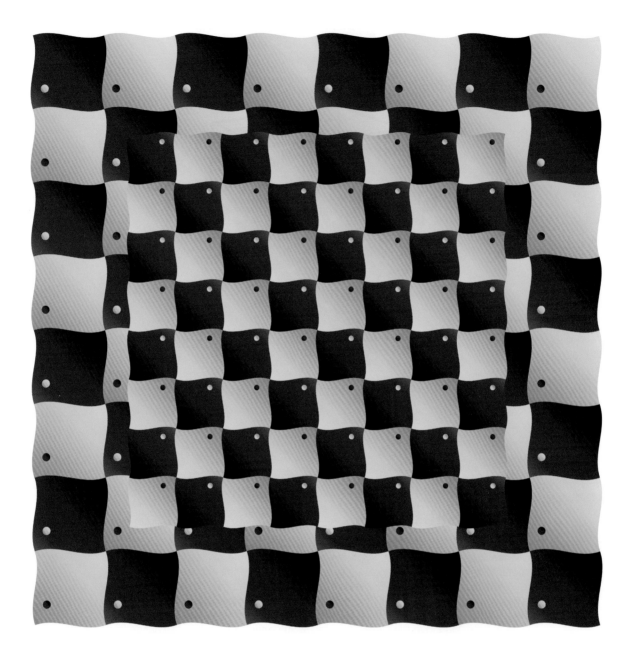

114, 115
Akiyoshi Kitaoka

Produced by Akiyoshi Kitaoka, a professor at the Ritsumeikan University in Kyoto who specialises in visual perception, these experimental images are intended to reveal quirks in the mechanical and cognitive systems that contribute to our personal perceptions of the world. Technically they're not art or design, they're science, pure and simple – psychology to be precise. But we don't have to justify ourselves; explaining why Akiyoshi Kitaoka is deserving of a place in this Annual is completely unneccesary. Just LOOK at those images. Now stop before you get dizzy.

Chidori; Ben Aki

ritsumei.ac.jp/kic/~akitaoka/index-e.html

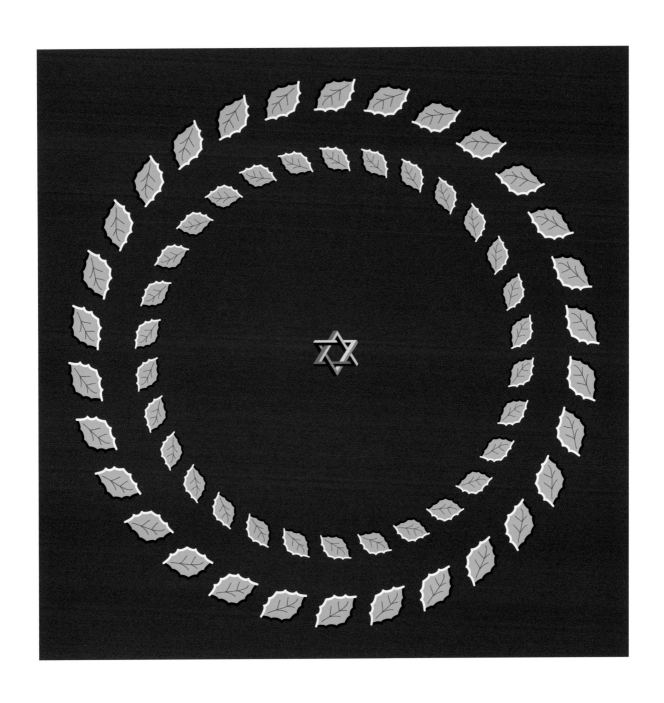

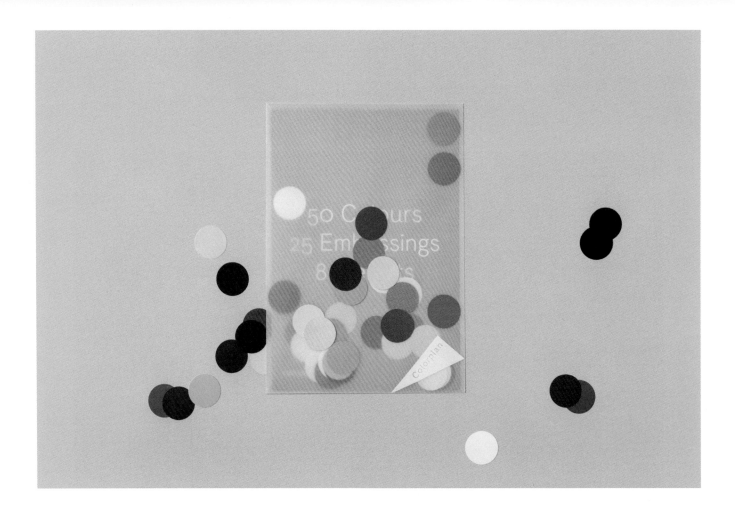

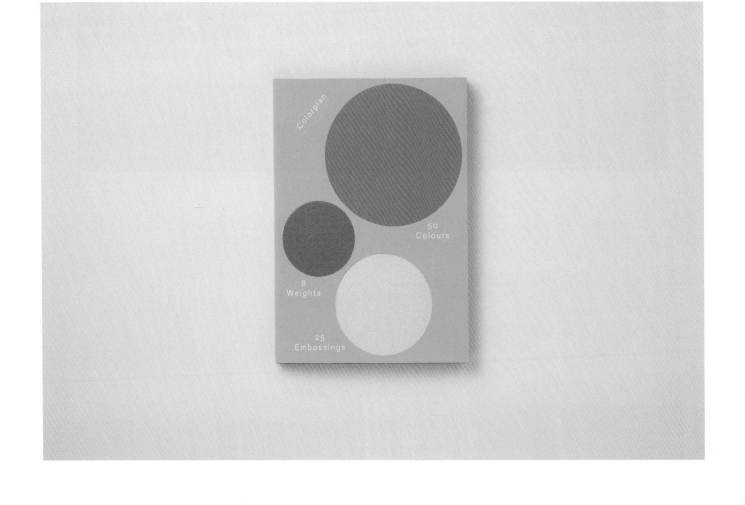

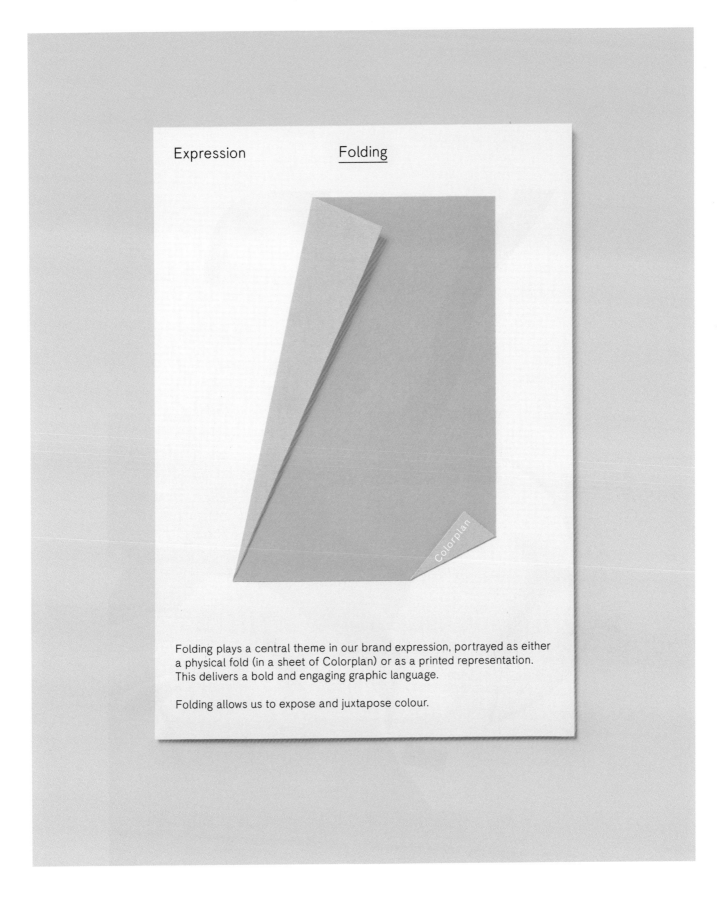

Expression   Folding

Folding plays a central theme in our brand expression, portrayed as either a physical fold (in a sheet of Colorplan) or as a printed representation. This delivers a bold and engaging graphic language.

Folding allows us to expose and juxtapose colour.

116, 117
Made Thought

When it comes to unadulterated design geekery, it's hard to beat a beautifully-designed paper sampler. Made Thought oversaw the redesign of the GF Smith Colorplan this year and had creatives everywhere drooling with their bright yet restrained treatment. If at its core design is about a combination of communication and beauty, then you'd be hard pushed to find a purer demonstration of this art from the past 12 months. For such a tactile triumph, there's also a surprisingly great digital version of this too, proving that Made Thought are at the peak of their powers.

madethought.com

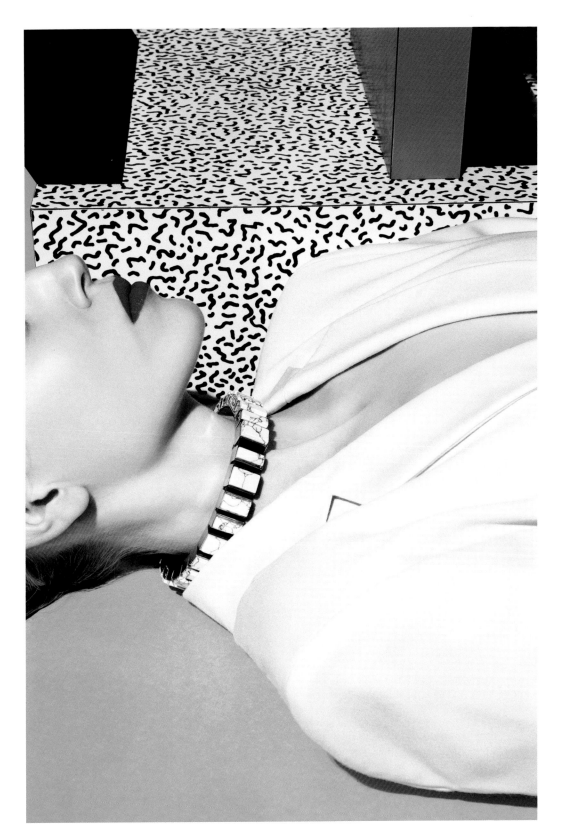

118, 119
Haw-lin

Nathan Cowen and Jacob Klein are the keepers of the secrets of Haw-lin, the guardians of that infinite scroll of aesthetic cool that has us cooing over 1990s denims, luxurious textures and washed-out fashion photography on a daily basis. Far more than being simple curators of cool, they've increasingly turned their talents to its creation too and their stint as stylists for the Süddeutsche Zeitung Magazin is testament to their ample capability to create stunning images from scratch with a refined eye for detail.

Photography: Haw-lin Services, Stylist: Almut Vogel

haw-lin.com

120, 121
HORT

True innovation within graphic design is a tricky thing to pull off in this day and age; what we used to digest in an hour is now gorged upon in mere seconds. Even so, folks like Eike König and his team at HORT are more than happy to ignore what everyone else is doing in the online image bank and as a result of this confidence, whenever they produce new work it always cuts a dash. This design for a techno collaboration between Marc Romboy and Ken Ishii, produced with photographer Michael Kohls was no different. Don't be surprised if HORT manage to find their way into every one of our Annuals for a good few years to come.

hort.org.uk

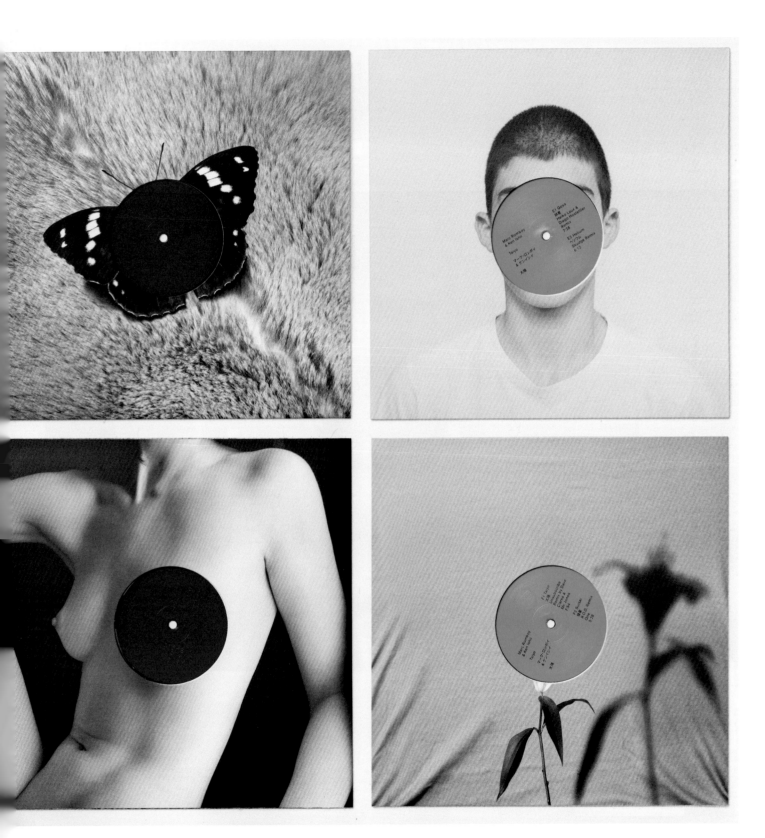

128, 129
Riitta Ikonen & Karoline Hjorth

We feel like Eyes As Big As Plates needs no explanation for its inclusion in these pages – the combination of exuberant geriatrics and nordic myth is enough to soften the stoniest of hearts. Knowing Riitta Ikonen as we do, we're also highly aware that she and Karoline Hjorth have invested months of research into the conceptual foundations of these simple and charming works. Digging deep into the unique mythologies of Riitta's hometown of Pohjois-Karjala, they've dressed their ageing neighbours in the costumes of Finnish folk characters and produced one of our favourite photographic series of the year.

Matti; Paul

eyesasbigasplates.wordpress.com

130, 131
Sarah Applebaum

If you don't like neon yetis and giant knitted sculptures then Sarah Applebaum probably isn't for you, but if that really isn't your flavour then put this book down at once – you've come to the wrong party. Sarah's a San Francisco native making brilliantly psychedelic, totally surreal art and illustration that distorts your sense of scale, perspective and reality. She makes little pairs of eyes that stare out of inky puddles on the floor, giant signs of ambiguous intent and exuberant rainbow-coloured sculptures that manage to lift a gloomy mood with ease. Disliking Sarah's work would be akin to despising happiness. It simply isn't possible.

Opposite page: *Space Signs*; Above: *Psychedelic Yetis* Photography: Hillary Hartley; Below: *Puddles*

sarahapplebaum.com

ÞÓRARINN ELDJÁRN

HÉR LIGGUR SKÁLD

132

Siggi Odds

Apparently Iceland (the country, not the shop) does magical things to humans – perhaps it's something in the large amount of auroras and puffin meat the inhabitants are exposed to. In illustrator Siggi Odds' case, the country seems to have brought him fabulous illustration skills. Siggi grew up in Vancouver, which explains the clear (although in some quarters controversial) influence of Native Canadian artwork on his own. Be it record sleeves, stamps or editorial work, this early inspiration is a constant feature in his portfolio, and makes it shine even brighter.

siggiodds.com

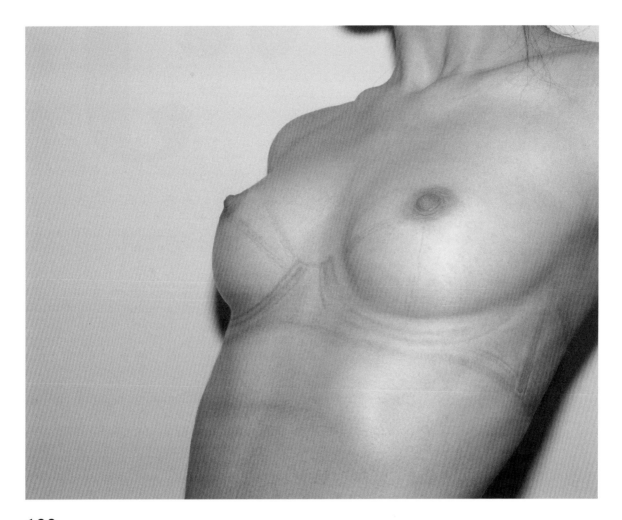

133

Scout Paré-Phillips

It's often difficult to find the halfway point between nudity and nakedness in contemporary photography, and fascination with the border which divides them is a popular point of contention. Scout Paré-Phillips' curiosity is with the residual imprints which stay on the body after the clothes which usually conceal it have been shed, and her photographs are beautifully simple in their sensual allure. There's a strange kind of darkness about her images too; undertones of restraint and control tinge the otherworldly paleness of her subject, which goes some way to explaining why we found ourselves so drawn to her work.

Bra

scoutparephillips.com

"Ja i Switze

pan

n

rland"

2013

136

Andy Massaccesi

What better man, I ask you, to make a book about discos than a man who has actually worked in them for eight years? Exactly. Milan-based photographer Andy Massaccesi (ever heard a name so apt for the dancefloor?) compiled a book of his own shots of crowds of revellers and from foam parties to festivals, discotheques to raves, this book's got it all. The best part is that you've been the person next to the topless guy wearing a lais or been stood surveying the scene before you, and Andy's is talented enough to capture something of these once-in-a-night-time experiences for ever.

Is Getting Over

andymassaccesi.com

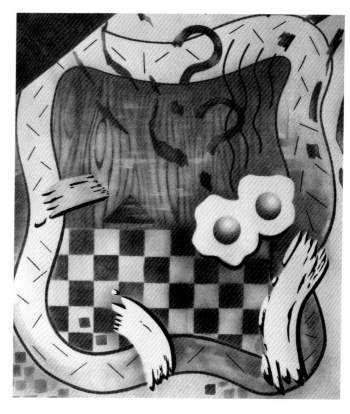

137
Brian Scott Campbell

Thank goodness Ohio-dwelling Brian Scott Campbell's parents ever met, because we are eternally thankful that he is alive. His charcoal drawings are infused with hot dogs, house plants, Greek tragedies and jazz, and his list of favourite word combinations on his website fills you up with inspiration like an unsuspecting balloon. The fact that he uses a medium such as charcoal to create these plentiful masterpieces is a feat in itself; whoever thought such a moody tool could produce so many laughs, and so much wonder?

Clockwise from bottom left *Party On; Chair, Hair; No Fun; Nude With Snowman*

brianscottcampbell.com

138
Damien Gilley

You can't go wrong with a bit of 3D painting that makes your brain have a sit-down chat with your retinas, and this is no exception. Damien lays strips of vinyl and latex against walls to create the kind of tunnel-vision landscape you'd more often see in old versions of Tron. His ability to completely alter our perspective of a surface – or the entire interior architecture of a gallery – in just a few lines is incredibly impressive, and baffling to say the least.

Fortress

damiengilley.com

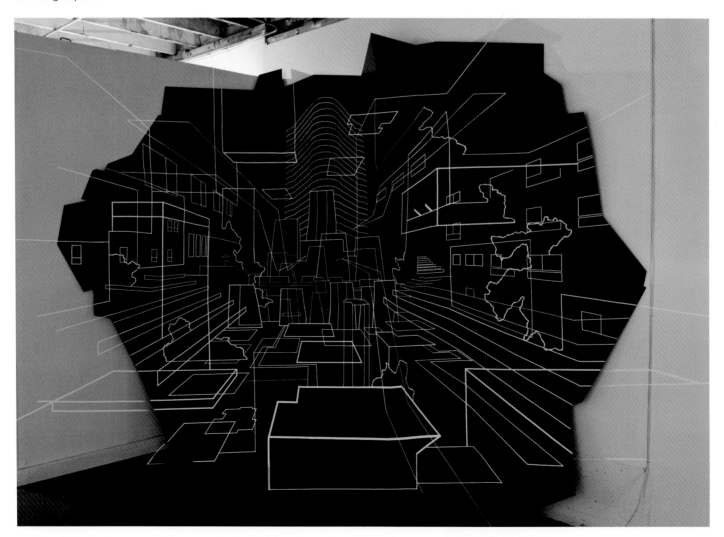

139

Joan Cornellà

Ugh, what isn't there to love about Joan Cornellà? Unless of course you're not really into gore, exceptionally dry toilet humour and comics. We don't know how we stumbled across Joan's work, but rest assured as soon as we did we were telling as many people we could about it. His simple, painted comic strips tell stories that you really have to be a bit sick in the head to invent. Luckily, Joan isn't deranged, he's just a really cool, nice guy from Barcelona. And the online world seems similarly smitten with his work as the 411,000 likes on his Facebook page testify (no big deal).

Hopity

elblogdejoancornella.blogspot.co.uk

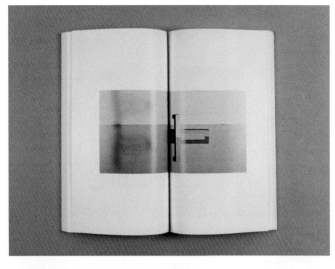

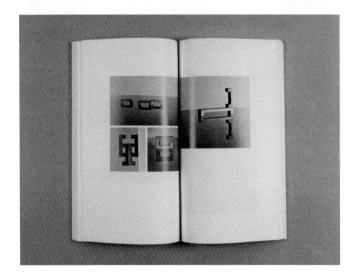

140
Polina Joffe

It's so pleasing when graphic designers have a recognisable style, and Polina Joffe's is certainly that although often the consistent thread is the methodological methods behind her eclectic portfolio. Each book she makes is conceptual, beautiful and intelligent; exploring the foggy line that divides aesthetically pleasing art and the enormous ideas behind it. One of Polina's publications looks into the relationship between the dot and the line, another just focuses on how great Kafka was. Fine by us. This is interesting, stylish and idea-driven graphic design from a young woman with a big future ahead of her.

Light Typographic Series

polinajoffe.com

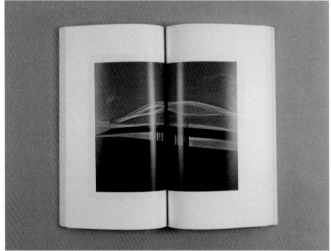

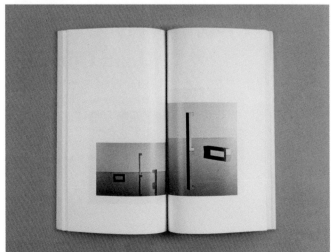

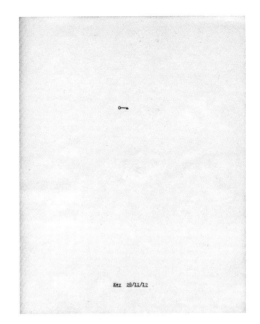

Key 28/11/12

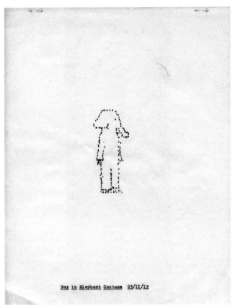

Boy in Elephant Costume 03/11/12

141
Michael Crowe
& Lenka Clayton

This meek little project went down an absolute storm on It's Nice That this year, maybe in part because we labelled it "perhaps the best project ever." But you know what? It kind of is. It's the quiet lovechild of the throbbing brains of Michael Crowe and Lenka Clayton, a project where they took turns in drawing a picture for each other every day for a month on a typewriter. The images they ended up creating are a kind of simple and romantic almanac that provide a glimpse into their respective creative minds.

lenkaclayton.co.uk, michaelcrowe.org

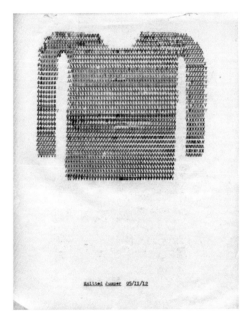

Knitted Jumper 05/11/12

This Typewriter 02/11/12

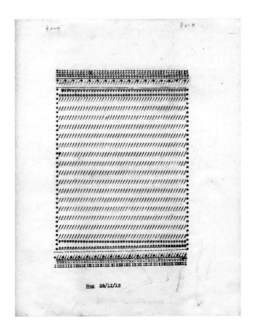

Rug 04/11/12

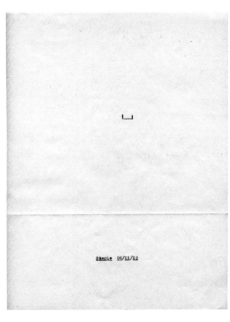

Staple 06/11/12

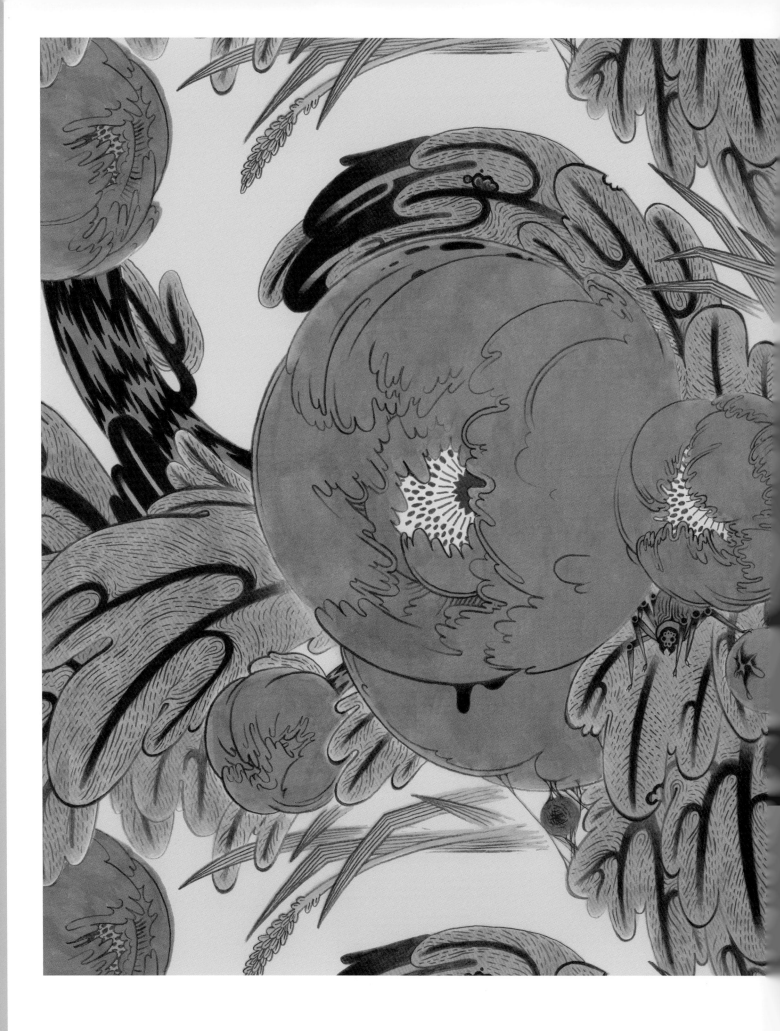

Micah Lidberg

It's testament to Micah Lidberg's inimitable skill that he can create illustrations of flowers that manage to look better than the real thing. His repeat patterns of peonies are plump, luxurious things on the cusp of bursting forth into bloom. At the same time they're dynamic; not like the floral patterns your mum used to wear on scarves but busy with movement and an energy that's present in all of Micah's work. I've seen peonies in real life, and they don't look anywhere near as good as this.

Peony

micahlidberg.com

Zoe Spawton

Projects born out of natural and genuine chance are the best kind in our eyes. In this case, Zoe Spawton decided to photograph a particularly dapper man named Ali whom she passed each day in Berlin, whose meticulous style continuously caught her eye. Knowing just how viral the project went made revisiting the blog a year on even more poignant – the blog posts are still regular and Ali, now a worldwide star, continued to dress sassily and walk down the same street each day. The fact that the hubbub is over and Ali's friendship with Zoe endures is enough to warm the cockles for years to come.

zoespawton.com

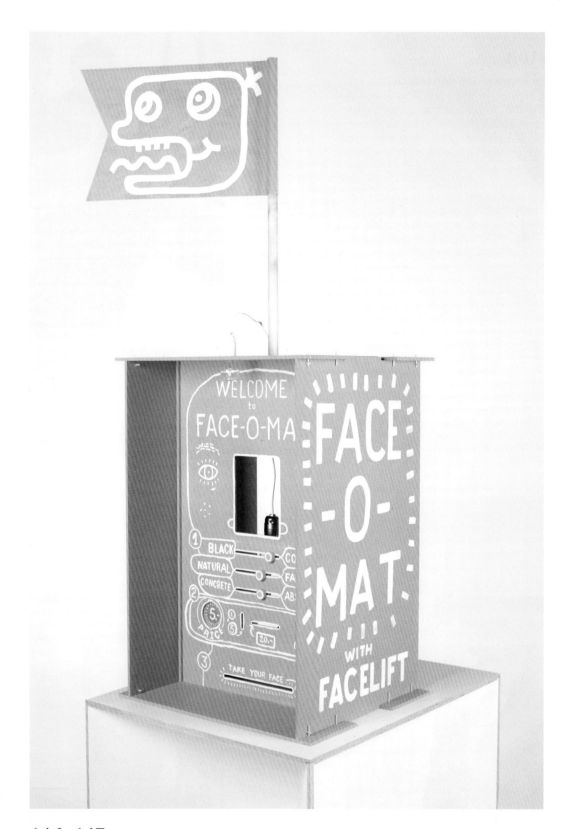

146, 147

Konstfack

As a rule this annual tends to focus on the work of individuals that we find to be particularly captivating, engaging or demonstrative of a specific skill set. Consequently there's not much work in here completed by groups of people, let alone large institutions. But we're happy to make an exception with Swedish design school Konstfack who seem to be churning out talent at a rate of knots. Whether you like the graphic weaves of Hannah Waldron, the eccentric illustration of Tobias Gutmann or Pål Rodenius' beautiful furniture design, it's impossible to deny the huge breadth of talent on display, and the consistency with which their graduates perform. Very impressive indeed.

Above: Tobias Gutmann: *Face-O-Mat;* Opposite: Lina Zedig and Pål Rodenius: *The Dhurrie Chair*

konstfack.se/milano/2013

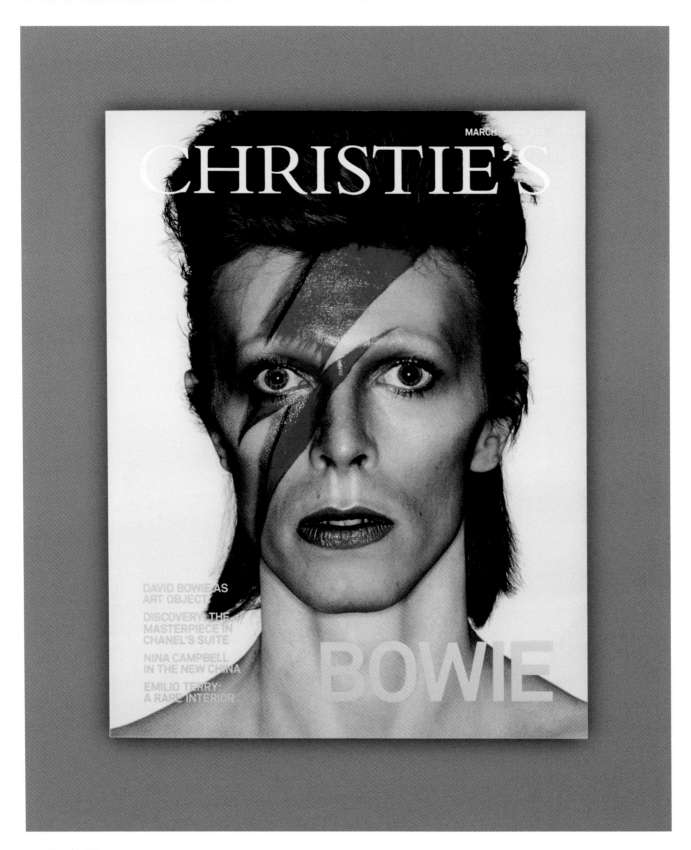

148, 149

Spin

Not being oil-rich oligarchs, the goings-on at the world's top auction houses have very little impact on our lives most of the time. But we were delighted to make an exception earlier this year when Tony Brooks and his Spin studio oversaw this eye-catching redesign for the Christie's magazine. Spin were actually tweaking their own designs, but the new set-up is terrific – powerful portrait-led covers, spacious, image-heavy layouts and some interesting type treatments all combine to impressive effect. So big thumbs-up. Wait no, that wasn't us bidding…

spin.co.uk

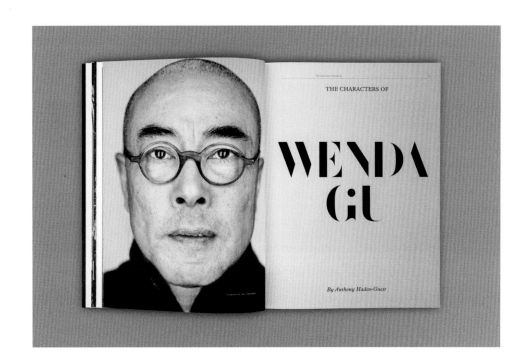

THE CHARACTERS OF

WENDA GU

By Anthony Haden-Guest

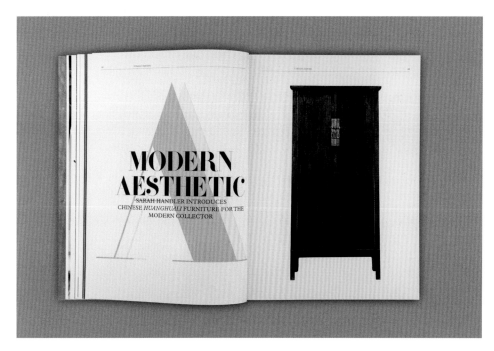

A MODERN AESTHETIC

SARAH HANDLER INTRODUCES
CHINESE *HUANGHUALI* FURNITURE FOR THE
MODERN COLLECTOR

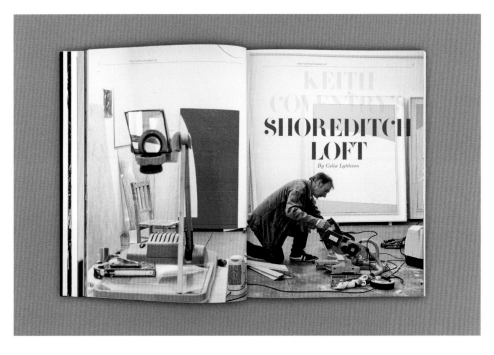

KEITH COVENTRY'S
SHOREDITCH LOFT

By Celia Lyttleton

"mu

ted"

2013

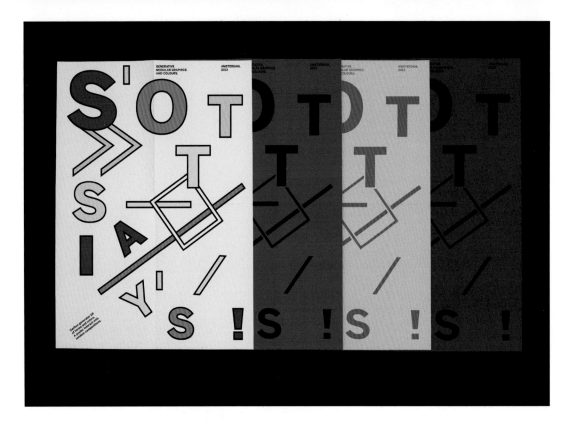

152

Ricardo Leite

Amsterdam-based Ricardo Leite is a graphic designer and art director who, with interactive design company Kaue Costa, has produced a software generator lovingly named Sottsays! The idea, inspired by the legendary Italian designer Ettore Sottsass, is simple – the generator formulates random compositions from a "kit of forms" resulting in a strangely harmonic series of twisted shapes and patterns with an inexplicable visual coherence. Ricardo has created a series of posters and booklets which demonstrate exactly what Sottsays! is capable of, and the randomly selected shapes and colours make for an impressive exploration of the role technology could play in the graphic design sphere.

rl85.com

153 → 154, 155

Baptiste Alchourroun

If there was one creative who bowled us over this year with their incredible aptitude for creating quietly brilliant images, it would have to be Baptiste Alchourroun. The French illustrator's labour-intensive coloured pencil drawings are in fact quite adult in their subject matter, while aesthetically masquerading as something from a children's book. No wonder a raft of big-name editorial clients have been beating a path to his door these past 12 months. And he's a dually gifted chap as his graphic design is impressive too, imbued with illustrative touches while maintaining a distinctly more figurative style.

Above: Why We Love Beautiful Things for The New York Times; Next page: For Article 11

alchourroun.fr

Christian Borstlap

Rather than hiding shyly behind the subtle shades of a visually anonymous brand identity, Christian Borstlap and his team at Part of a Bigger Plan decided to embrace a vibrant, unique and visually striking identity when rebranding Rhiannon Pickles PR. The result is based around 23 colourful illustrations which use circles to reinterpret work by the creatives represented by the firm, and it is geometric without seeming staid; beautifully executed without being flashy. Here's an identity for a cultural PR brand which is a work of art in its own right.

partofabiggerplan.com

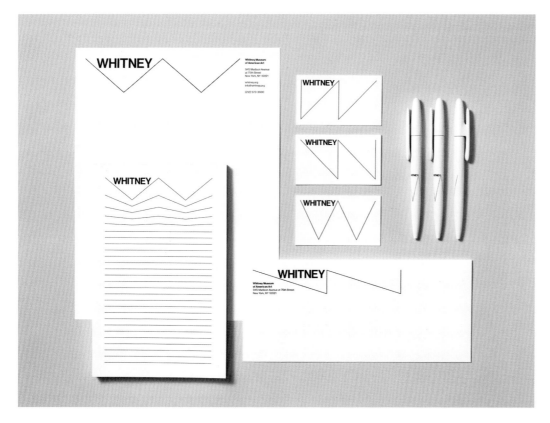

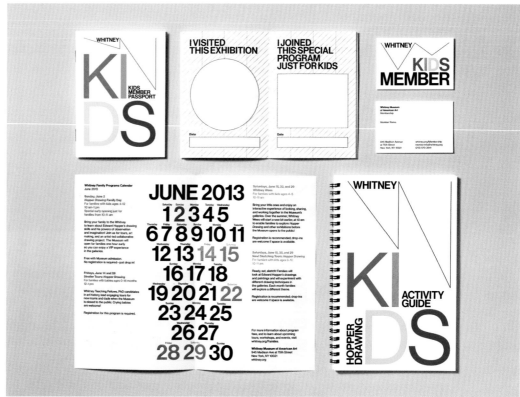

157

Experimental Jetset

The approaching expansion of the Whitney Museum necessitated an update of the institution's identity; a daunting task for certain. But Amsterdam-based studio Experimental Jetset took up the gauntlet with brio. The brilliant new design works around the malleability of the letter "W", a bold, confident symbol that can be re-imagined and reinterpreted to suit the museum's diverse needs from a fun new perspective. The Whitney's embrace of such a fluid identity resonates with its ambition as an institution dedicated to the contemporary, while the playfulness which runs throughout the stationery ensures accessibility as well. A perfect pairing.

experimentaljetset.nl

158, 159
Jack Hudson & Lord Whitney

There are few creative projects which are worthy of puns as conspicuous as Mock 'N' Roll, but fortunately Jack Hudson's collaboration with Lord Whitney on this series of fictional record covers was a more than adequate match for the wordplay. Weird and wonderful with a compelling visual vernacular which runs threadlike through the series in spite of its bizarre diversity, the project is a fun homage to the colour-saturation of record shop shelves from years gone by. So thrown on some Bobby Coolfinger and let's get this party started!

jack-hudson.com, lordwhitney.co.uk

BOBBY COOLFINGER

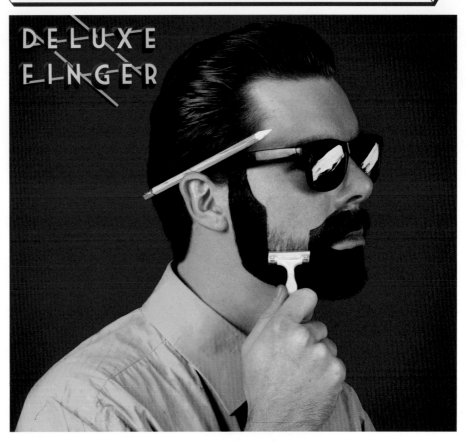

DELUXE FINGER

LES TROIS ANORAKS
LA BALEINE!

161, 162
Luke Evans

When it comes to Luke Evans' work, things are most definitely not what they seem. Don't believe me? In Forge, what appears to the uninformed eye to be a series of vast post-apocalyptic landscapes and cruel rocky coastlines is in fact a carefully assembled mini-set composed of salt, sand, smoke, careful lighting and no small amount of visual deception. Still a student, Luke's eye for visually arresting detail and concentration of effect onto a tiny set is more than enough reason for us to gawp at his artistic skill. We'd stake good money on this young man making (more) waves in years to come.

Forge II

luk-e.com

162

Nadja Staubli

Swiss photographer Nadja Staubli can, we imagine, light up any environment she steps into. Her natural affinity to emphasise the colours which occur organically all around us – but which are so often overlooked simply because we are busy looking down – is somewhat eery. A whole series of warmly-lit coral tones, acidic greens and striking cobalt blues resonate throughout her images as though infected with the kind of high saturation usually found only on the Disney Channel. The result is that her photographs are paradoxically both vibrant and still at the same time.

Community

nadjastaubli.com

163
Philipp Meyer

In a fascinating new scrutiny of the limitations of interaction design, Philipp Meyer has created a tactile comic which seeks to make the joy of graphic fiction as accessible and exciting for the blind and partially sighted as it is for the rest of us. The form relies upon a kind of sequential tactile storytelling which reinvents the comic panel through embossed images and perforation, and is notable as much for its sincere intent as for its aesthetic appeal. Needless to say this is a long-overdue undertaking which will hopefully open up the joys of comic fiction to anybody who might wish to read it.

Life

hallo.pm

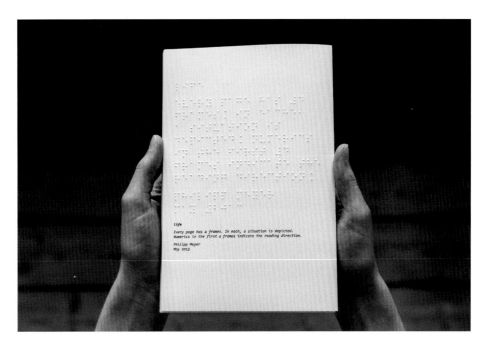

164, 165
Nolan Conway

Fast-food behemoth McDonalds is often the subject of a barrage of criticism but one one saving grace amid this sea of disparagement is that it is one of few places in America where the poor and the rich dine side by side without prejudice. Nolan Conway is both recognising and championing this diversity with his brilliant series The People You Meet at McDonalds, which revels in the accidental alignment of race, age, occupation and character on the famous moulded plastic chairs. Not only are the images hilarious, but his tone combines the kind of gently probing Horatian satire with humour in a way that's completely timeless in its appeal.

Ralph and Lia Whitefoot and their dog, Pretty Boy,
Yakima, Washington

nolanconway.com

166, 167
Yolanda Dominguez

Only gifted artists can take terrible events from the comfortable distance of newspaper pages and re-situate them within their viewers' immediate surroundings, and that's precisely how Yolanda Dominguez' photography functions. Her project Fashion Victims came in the aftermath of the collapse of a textile factory in Bangladesh this year, in which more than 1,000 workers were killed. By recreating the horror of that event in miniature, posing models beneath piles of rubble in Madrid's most famous shopping street, Yolanda forces her audience to question their own role in the abuse of cheap labour, and hammers home just how implicated in injustice the Western world really is.

yolandadominguez.com

Gradua

tes 2013

5/6   La Jolla Road   A.T. 2013

170

Alice Tye

Alice Tye is based in south-east London, but her heart lies way over on the west coast of the USA if her work is anything to go by. She studied illustration at Camberwell but has worked with paint and lithography to create her Californian scenes, re-imagined through the prism of how America's golden coast is presented to us by the films, TV shows and books which immortalise it.

Her lithographs hum with an unsettling tension – that behind the sunny facades lies something darker – her four-metre long concertina fold-book of La Jolla Road in Palm Springs created via Google Street View images does likewise. Her dissertation project started with the premise: "Is modernist architecture used as visual shorthand for malevolent characters in popular films?" and she has recreated scenes from the likes of Diamonds Are Forever and LA Confidential with real flair.

171
Bianca Tuckwell

Farnham graduate Bianca Tuckwell is fascinated by organic structures – from British birds' nests in The Growth that is Our Own Cradle, to Land, a beautiful study of a farm in New South Wales. Both align actual nature with human nature in a way which avoids both the sentimentality of straight-up portraiture and the impersonality of barren landscape photography.

For somebody so young to already have settled upon this magical equation is unusual to see, and Bianca executes the careful balance beautifully. Her Ryder project is equally interesting, as it sees the structure of a bicycle visually dismantled into a representative series of lines, shapes and details which are then grouped together and isolated on a frame – calling up ideas of altered contexts in a really neat design.

174

Edward Cheverton

Brighton graduate Edward Cheverton first came to our attention when he won our Student of the Month competition in March 2012 after he wowed us with his truly fantastic jazz collages. What we love about Edward's style is how he's not afraid to show of all his working-out and sketches, which when pieced together tell a pleasing story of colour, sound and, most importantly, fun.

Moving away from making projects based solely around jazz, Edward went on to create colourful zines and prints full of characters so sweet and funny they're almost begging to be animated. It was great not only to showcase his considerable talents but to see the progress he made during his last year of study.

cargocollective.com/edwardcheverton

THEE TTRIP

175

Edward Monaghan

Edward Monaghan is very much his own man. Upon arriving at Central Saint Martins three years ago he quickly decided that the prescriptive nature of his illustration course was not especially to his tastes and so he set about creating an extraordinary body of illustration and comics in a style that's reached a level of refinement well beyond his years.

Edward's work stands out initially for its vibrant colour; huge, busy compositions that are bursting with purples, greens and yellows. On close inspection however, there's a lot more going on after that initial visual punch. Edward's become something of a master at reductive storytelling, creating complex narratives with a few simple lines that make an increasing amount of sense the more you stare at them. That said he's also a dab-hand at cramming as much information into a single frame as humanly possible.

edwardcarvalhomonaghan.co.uk

176
Lottie Brzozowski

Every year when we scour through the hundreds of submissions to The Graduates, we come across a great many graphic design students whose final projects bear little relation to traditional ideas of the craft. But there is also a place for great graphic design talent of a more traditional bent, such as Lottie Brzozowski.

The Liverpool John Moores graduate combined impressive ideas with flawless execution and has a really natural feel for the communicative power of great-looking, tactile work. She is aware of dominant industry trends without slavishly following them – a major way of discerning the best from the rest. We were particularly enamoured by her risograph work as well as her experimental typeface Vertex – "created by a system of folding which disrupted a 2D surface, making it appear 3D."

lottiebrzozowski.co.uk

177

Juliana Futter

London College of Communication graduate Juliana Futter is an illustrator par excellence with a penchant for the strange, surreal and the downright filthy. We have a special place in our hearts reserved for illustration that pushes the boundaries of simple aesthetic pleasantry, and Juliana's playful renderings of grotesque religious mythology do just that.

In terms of subject matter Juliana favours the archaic over the contemporary, producing work that's influenced by ancient creation myths, the Surrealist practice of interpreting dreams and the fabrication of her own personal religious lexicon (it's based around cosmic eggs). But her image-making is a combination of traditional and contemporary practices, incorporating ceramics, screen-printing and gouache alongside Photoshop, Illustrator and a website filled with charming gifs.

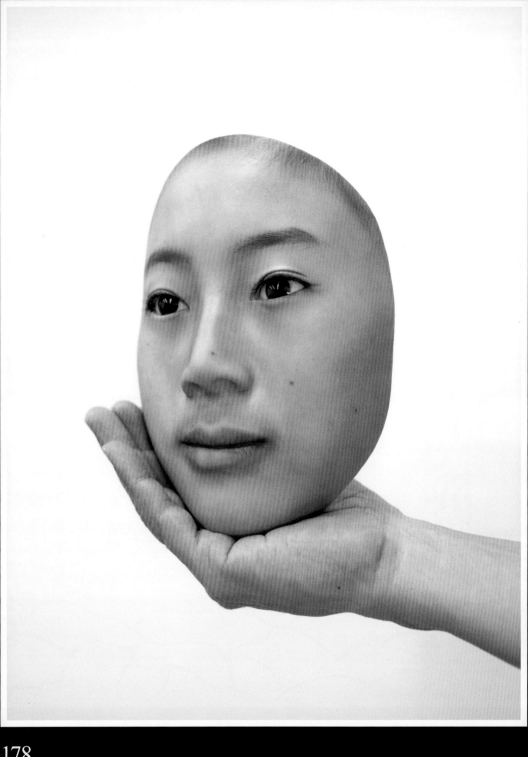

178

Luisa Whitton

Photographer Luisa Whitton is a serious Japanophile. When she's not walking the streets of Osaka and Tokyo capturing locals doing their thing, she's deep within the country's robotic research facilities cataloguing the synthetic faces, mechanical arms and cold, dead stares of the very latest in technological innovation. The robot interest has also come into play in another personal project that's seen her hack an Xbox Kinect to make it into a rudimentary photographic device.

She spent two years abroad during her degree at the London College of Communication, working on personally motivated projects that she's strategically incorporated into her coursework. In doing so, she gained a better understanding of how to make work outside the confines of education; a skill that every graduate should really possess when they pick up their diploma. Most don't though, which set Luisa apart from many of her peers.

cargocollective.com/luisawhitton

179
Matthew Hill

Kingston's graphic design course has secured a reputation for excellence and 2013 was no different thanks to talents like Matthew Hill. He doesn't just think outside the box; he's more than willing to clamber outside of the box and get his hands dirty coming up with new and innovative design solutions.

His work ranges from the downright fun – a triangular ping pong table that you can arrange in about 100 different ways to play with all your friends at the same time, with brilliant and weirdly-shaped bats – to the intriguing and decidedly more serious fire extinguisher-come-champagne bottle, a well-made comment on the amount of house fires caused by alcohol abuse. In case you needed further proof that this is a brain to admire, his Signature project played on the growing importance of digital interfaces with a mechanical printer which had been altered to give it the ability to portray a degree of personality through "hand-written" signatures.

Everything in the world has its own spirit which
can be released by setting it into vibration.
- Oskar Fischinger

180
Oliver Jennings

Oliver Jennings was hands-down the most unusual of this year's crop of graduates. Having spent three years studying graphic design at Camberwell College of Art, you'd expect him to have emerged with a couple of tasteful publications, some posters and maybe a handful of album covers, but you'd be wrong. Instead he's been experimenting with strange sonic landscapes, exploring the natural sounds present in everyday objects, from house plants to giant river-spanning bridges.

There's some complex theory behind his work and more than a dash of influence from the hive-mind of Youtube – his sound installations derive inspiration from a large collection of pseudo-scientific experiments that exist as video tutorials online – and we were incredibly impressed by his confidence. There's not many people bold enough to spend three years playing with sound obsessively when they should be mastering InDesign.

cargocollective.com/isnessarmy

181
Charlie Patterson

Charlie Patterson studied graphic design at Chelsea, and in keeping with that instutions's reputation he has a predictably good grounding in the fundamental skills. But where Charlie's portfolio really stood out was through his playful and interesting ideas.

The Creative Club was a project that rewarded design professionals for their skills by handing out charming personalised merit badges (and acted as a heck of a networking tool to boot), while Charlie's LEGO ads for the YCN briefs really tapped into the toy's imaginative potential. Working with Jasper Van Den Bosch, Charlie also won the Southbank Centre's BOOST programme for their simple, stylish, geometric bike decorations.

charlieoscarpatterson.com

"These guys your rules, daring enc them, they' let you n the rules

don't play by
out if you're
ugh to join
e willing to
t play by
either…"

2013

186

Peter Chadwick

If a great idea and clever name is all you need to achieve design brilliance then we imagine Peter Chadwick of Popular is basking in the warm glow of creative success right now. His Desktop Publishing project consists of a plain MDF and steel table customised with spaces for ink tubs, a glass mixing area and four plates for each stage of your CMYK print process. His little plate printing table is a simple piece of kit but turns out some truly lovely results. It looks beautiful, functions fantastically and has a pun for a title. Three thumbs up from us!

Photography: David Ryle

popularuk.com

187

Charles Burns

In the year that McSweeney's literary magazine The Believer celebrated its tenth anniversary, it would be indecent not to celebrate its outrageously talented cover artist. Although the anniversary edition actually didn't make use of his illustrations, Charles Burns has adorned nearly every Believer cover since its inception, rendering characters as diverse as Fidel Castro and Joan Didion, Luciano Pavarotti and Devendra Banhart in his unmistakable style. We'd celebrate Charles' work any day of the week but for ten years of loyal service to one of the best mags around his achievements absolutely have to be acknowledged.

Alan Moore

adambaumgoldgallery.com/burns_charles

188, 189
Peder Norrby

In last year's Annual we featured artist Jenny Odell who harvested various features like water slides and swimming pools from Google Maps and collected them together. This year our online-map-based contribution comes from Peder Norrby and his amazing collection of iOS Glitches. Whereas Jenny's project was built on these tools' comprehensive coverage, Peder celebrates instead those moments when the system breaks down. The surreal scenes he's amassed on his Flickr account show what happens when artificial intelligence fails to cope with the complex nuances of reality and we are left with an Inception-style world of melting roads and shifting buildings.

flickr.com/photos/pedernorrby

190, 191
Kim Keever

There's a handful of people in this book whose work we knew would be included as soon as we found them. Kim Keever is one such creative. For the sheer meticulousness of process, the utter absurdity of scale and the visually arresting results, Kim deserves an enormous amount of respect. He creates his otherworldly landscapes inside 200 gallon tanks of water, throwing pigments and paint into the liquid to create extraordinary backdrops. It's a slow process and requires an enormous amount of trial and error before the final result is captured on a Hasselblad. It takes a heck of a lot of work but we have no doubt that it's absolutely worth it.

Above: *Studio view for Waterfalls;* Opposite: *Mountains*

kimkeever.com

192
Léo Caillard

Every now and then we come across a project with which we become smitten; immediately and completely. This year that accolade goes to Léo Caillard's Hipster In Stone series, which basically does what it says on the tin. Léo had the idea while walking through the Louvre and after photographing various statues, he then hunted down models with corresponding physiques. These he shot in archetypal hipster attire, with lighting designed to resemble museum conditions. With the help of retoucher Alexis Persani the pictures were combined and the results, as you can see, are terrific.

leocaillard.com

193

Matthew Craven

There's a lot of work featured on It's Nice That which is impressive partly because of the sheer amount of time it must have taken, and Matthew Craven is right up there with the most meticulous of them. The Brooklyn-based artist's enormous, totemistic prints are like the tantalising marks left by a lost civilisation, simultaneously nonsensical and pregnant with apparent meaning. His is an enjoyably diverse portfolio with recurring interests in shape, pattern and symbolism, as well as an apparent taste for leaving the viewer not quite sure what's what.

Life Totem I

matthewcraven.com

194

Michelle Matson

New Jersey-based sculptor Michelle Matson once appeared on an American reality TV show called Work of Art: The Next Great Artist which is brilliant but not quite as brilliant as her work which came crashing into our lives back in June. She studied at the prestigious School of Visual Arts in New York but her work has a vibrancy and a sense of humour which we would suggest is unteachable. You're spoiled for choice perusing her portfolio but these Flower Girl sculptures embody her combination of playful ideas and technical execution which tickles us so much.

michellematson.tv

195

Mohammadreza Mirzaei

There's two broad kinds of street photography – the simple, point-and-shoot variety where a single moment is captured with spontaneous excellence and then the kind where the photographer places their own unique filter on the scene they show, turning an everyday image into something altogether more striking and ethereal. Mohammadreza Mirzaei takes the second kind of photographs, documenting views from bus windows, shadowed hallways and coastal walkways and impregnating them with a tangible sense of the unreal. He does this either through a subtle over-saturation of colour or portentous swathes of darkness that threaten to encroach on the subject of the image. The end result is nothing short of magical.

Stammer

mrmirzaei.com

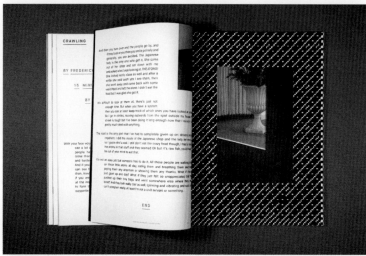

196

Flaneur Magazine

The rise of independent magazines – hailed by some as a new golden age of print – has thrown up some enjoyably niche topics on which titles concentrate. Take Flaneur magazine which launched this year with its focus is on a single street. For its inaugural issue this was Kanstrasse in Berlin which they explored with the help of artists, writers, designers and photographers to create a really fascinating portrait of this eclectic road. Add in exceptional, content-supporting design from Michelle Phillips and Johannes Conrad of Y-U-K-I-K-O and you've got one of our favourite new tomes of the past year.

flaneur-magazine.com

Rob Hunter

It's a deeply satisfying experience to watch a creative whose work you admire develop and grow with each new commission. Rob Hunter has been on our radar for a good few years now and we were deeply enamoured with his first graphic novel The New Ghost, a charming tale of a rookie spirit learning how to be dead. This year he managed to surpass himself with his second shot at graphic storytelling, releasing the infinitely more complex Map of Days. Here Rob pushes the narrative medium further than he's attempted before, resulting in a work that feels experienced and mature without losing that playful sense of experimentation which we've come to expect from this incredibly talented fellow.

Published by Nobrow

robertfrankhunter.com

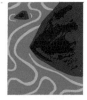

198, 199 ← 200

Thomas Prior

Breaking the rules is fun, and fireworks are really fun, so breaking rules with fireworks must be the most fun you can have. We wouldn't know, we don't play with fire, but Thomas Prior's photos of a firework fight in Mexico arguably look like one of the best ways to spend an evening, so long as you don't value your personal safety at all. The rest of Thomas' portfolio isn't short on excitement either, featuring shots of sandstorms, firearms, explosions and extreme surfing, but these images capture the raw energy of Tultepec with incredible flair and they're unlike anything else we've ever seen.

March 8, Tultepec, Mexico

thomasprior.com

201
Tim Lahan

Masterful New York-based illustrator Tim Lahan has become a firm favourite of ours thanks to his fun, bright and communicative style. Named one of the prestigious Young Guns by the Art Director's Club last year, Tim has shown just why he is so highly rated over the past 12 months with a host of great work for the likes of The New Yorker, McSweeney's and The National. His work rate is tremendous, his consistency incredible and his eye for a killer image is seemingly going from strength to strength. No wonder the man's so in demand really.

Italian Food for Lucky Peach

timlahan.com

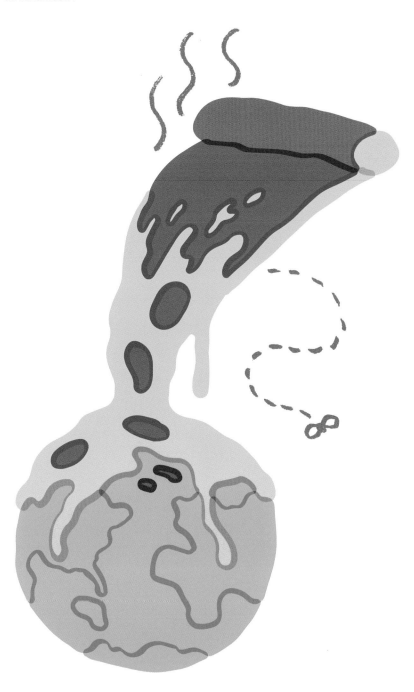

"Armeni
Quar

al Cattle ...te..ly"

204, 205
Bronia Stewart

It takes a keen eye to create images which confront the media's sexualisation of women without preaching to deaf ears, but that's exactly what Bronia Stewart managed to achieve when she spent nine months photographing behind the scenes at Babestation, the adult entertainment TV channel. Focussing on the affectionate and sociable atmosphere on set, Bronia's shots are candid without slipping into voyeurism, emphasising the themes of aspiration and ambition which underpin the series rather than the girls who star in it. All of which makes for a startlingly brilliant first project from a young photographer, who we suspect has much more to offer yet.

broniastewart.com

206

Content Aware Typography

We love glitches of all shapes and sizes. The idea of technology messing up and falling flat on its face is just appealing, kind of like when the cleverest kid in school drops his pencil case – you enjoy it, right? Perhaps that's why there's so much joy to be found in this blog which invites people to take famous logos, drag them into Photoshop and refill them entirely with the Content Aware tool. The results are melted, glitchy blobs of colour that are like the punk Frankenstein's monster of the Adobe Suite.

contentawaretypography.tumblr.com

207

Damien Cuypers

Blame it on the rising temperatures if you will, but there were a couple of weeks this year when things on the website got a little bit...sexy. The Anonymous Sex Journal played no small part; in fact, publisher Alex Tieghi-Walker and his partner in crime illustrator Damien Cuypers might even be responsible, seeing as their study of intimate and naughty first-time revelations got the heart rates rising. Damien turned his terrific talents to providing the accompanying visuals for these tantalising readers' tales striking the perfect balance between saucy and silly.

damienflorebertcuypers.com

208, 209
Ed Piskor

Ed Piskor has a real comic book pedigree but it's his most recent project which got us really excited. Hip Hop Family Tree is a huge collection of comics providing an illustrated insight into the the early days of the musical genre, documenting Grandmaster Flash, Afrika Bambaataa and Kurtis Blow (among others) and their blistering rise to stratospheric fame. We can't think of a medium more apt to document the "viral propagation of a culture" than the comic book, and the combination of this one's quality with its subject matter ensures it will play an irreplaceable role on bookshelves for a long time yet.

edpiskor.com

210

Drury Brennan

Jazz drummer turned artist Drury Brennan is in no hurry to let go of his musical fervour, and his natural affinity for combining his two great passions has led him to merge his love of syncopated music with graphic art. He makes a very compelling case for the similarities between the two, based on a shared conviction of gesture and sense of improvisation, which he then deconstructs in the course of creating his huge striking works. If the intricate typographic constructions he has produced are anything to go by, jazz and calligraphy go together very well indeed.

Word Jazz

drurybrennan.com

211

Maciek Pozoga

A great many photographers stick to what they know when it comes to their craft and that's understandable; whether they predominantly shoot landscapes or portraits there's often a clear running theme throughout what and how they shoot. Not with Maciek Pozoga though. His photographs range from smouldering volcanoes, to cool bands, to chickens, to Tolkien-esque ramblers. His unpredictable flair for photographing what no one else does, or can, might leave you with your jaw on the desk in front of you.

Clockwise from bottom left:
Il Serpentone; Anonymous Smiley Engraving; Voyages Extraordinaires; Pilgrim; Stromboli

maciekpozoga.tumblr.com

212, 213
Fredrik Åkum

In perfect compliance with our stereotypical love of complaining about good weather, us Brits were both horrified and overjoyed to be hit with a stifling heatwave this summer. In the midst of the sweatpatches, the bickering over fans and the hiding miserably in the shade, Fredrik Åkum graced us with his artwork. The Swedish painter and photographer effortlessly creates images which encapsulate all the best elements of summer; the haze of heat rising from the ground, the tropical foliage and the gauzy palette of childhood holidays. Now that we're done complaining about it, this creative wizard has us longing for some sunshine. Typical.

Plants; Anna-Lotta & Found Leaf

fredrikakum.com

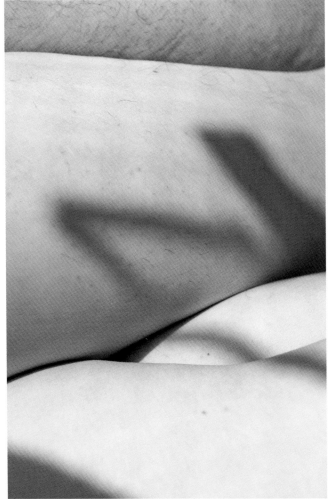

214, 215
Go Itami

As often as Japan crops up in our daily lives – in the products we use, the technology we covet, the news we read – its sheer exoticism can sometimes make it feel very removed from Western culture. This symbolic distance is purely imagined of course, and photographer Go Itami is doing a brilliant job of shattering the illusion. His images possess an obscure stillness; whether he is reducing an entire city to a peaceful silence, casting a softly dappled glowing light over perpetually rippling water or simply offering a brief but poignant glimpse into a world utterly unknown to us and yet strikingly normal to him. Few photographers have so successfully struck so quiet a chord in what is often seen as so noisy a culture.

goitami.jp

216

HTML Flowers

It's pretty hard to find such heart-on-sleeve, tender work as HTML Flowers', or for that matter any that is so meticulously drawn in such a unique style. The artist (whose real name is Grant Gronewold) lives in Australia, and spends his time making wild music, writing poetry and updating his blog with new incredible comics and drawings to the delight of his network of ardent fans. Grant's something of a messiah in the niche, online community of off-the-wall, life-affirming art, and you can see why. He's magical.

Hind The Shrubs for Fleshtonez Erotic Comix Exhibtition at Paradise Hills Gallery, Melbourne

htmlflowers.tumblr.com

217
Stephen Teeuw

Accomplished painter Stephen Teeuw's portfolio features portraits, animals and landscapes brimming with life and vibrancy. So when we stumbled across a secret page on his website, entitled Things I Shouldn't Have Drawn, we were intrigued, then gleeful. Huge women with their breasts draped across tables, a scrotum with a head and two penises attached, a man squatting over a face, you get the idea. Utter filth and complete gold, as far as squandered artistic gifts are concerned. Pat on the back to you Stephen.

Clockwise from bottom left:
Cats; A Mother; Sick; Your Fucking Face

stephenteeuw.co.uk

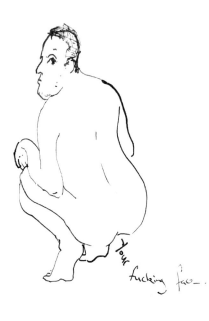

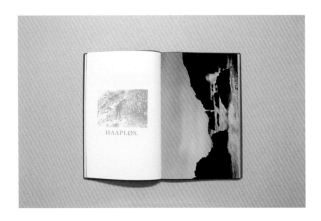

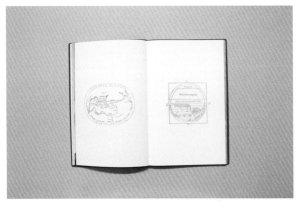

218

Freddy Dewe Matthews

Bouvetøya is the most remote island in the world; owned by Norway, it has an area of 49 square kilometres. Small groups throughout history have undertaken voyages to the island, often believing that something spiritual occurs to humans when they spend time there. Artist Freddy Dewe Matthews dedicated a few years of his life to researching this weird place, and made an informative and aesthetically pleasing book collating his findings. With interviews, maps and very readable discoveries all bound in a beautifully-designed little publication, this is one of the best books we've seen this year.

Bouvetøya: A Cultural History of an Isolated Landmass (Design: Jasmine Raznahan (ARPA) and Xavier Poultney)

freddydewematthews.com

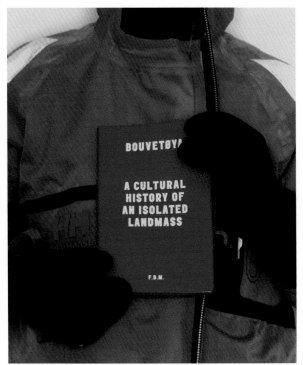

219

McCann Copenhagen

Most of the discourse around the advertising world this past year has, not surprisingly, been defined by digital. How great it was then to come across a campaign which reminded the world of the power the unfashionable billboard can still wield. To celebrate Black Sabbath's first record in 35 years, the McCann Copenhagen agency decided to dig through layers of billboard posters and expose menacing Black Sabbath posters beneath, just to quietly remind everyone that the band have been lurking beneath the surface of modern day trashy music, and they're back with a vengeance. Incredible..

mccann.dk

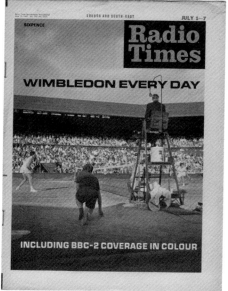

220, 221
Radio Times

How many publications can you name which truly span several generations? Sadly they're thin on the ground in a digital culture which relentlessly pursues the new, but this year's Museum of London exhibition to celebrate the 90th birthday of the Radio Times reminded us just how grand a role this British institution has played over the past century. The covers on show documented almost a century of British history, from the reign of comedy king Charlie Chaplin, to the Swinging Sixties, sweeping in two World Wars and several changes in the Royal Family the meantime. Here's to the next ten, Radio Times!

museumoflondon.org.uk

"perha
could sn
dough
than r

ps you
nack the
rather
oll it…"

2013

FOLLOW
ME ON
TWITTER
London Borough of
Hackney
COMMERCIAL WASTE SERVICES
CONTINENTAL 1100
0208 356 6683

226, 227

Ian Stevenson

In Craig Damrauer's excellent New Math project, "Modern art = I could do that + Yeah but you didn't." Ian Stevenson is one of the finest examples of this maxim, with work that is funny, silly and (in technical terms) terrifically simple. Daubing the phrase "Follow Me On Twitter" on a wheelie bin isn't difficult, but the kind of creative mind that conceives of it as a project and recognises its potential as a satire on our social media-obsessed society is both rare and well worth celebrating.

Twitter; Art

ianstevenson.co.uk

228, 229
Isabella Rozendaal

Isabella Rozendaal, who wowed us this year with her project Isabella Hunts, is a rare creature in the world of documentary photographers. Her work is confrontational, controversial and researched to a breathtaking degree (she expects this project to last for a minimum of six years), and has led her to travel the world in pursuit of a new historical and cultural understanding of the practice of hunting. As she explains: "I was intrigued by this combination of a peaceful, meditative interaction with nature and the unforgiving confrontation with death." As were we, as we rapidly became absorbed in the stunning yet unforgiving nature of her images.

Clockwise from bottom left: *Dog With Hare, Holland; Mojo's First Duck Hunt, Oregon; Russian Wolf Hound, Abu Dhabi*

isabellarozendaal.com

230, 231

Jan Buchczik

Coming across Jan's work was like unearthing some kind of glorious treasure from the soil of the internet. Fresh colours, crisp lines and not one dud image in the whole portfolio, Jan's work kind of knocked us sideways this year. His work is a friendlier take on Julian Opie, with some images of doner kebabs, wonky toupées and Annie Hall references thrown in for good measure. It's rare we stumble across a creative talent whose work stops us in our tracks, but Jan goes down as one of our best discoveries of the past 12 months.

Heads Up; A Way of Seeing (above)

buchczik.tumblr.com

232, 233
Jen Osborne

As much as we love photographers who beautifully capture the mundane, how about a photographer who beautifully captures the weird and the wonderful? Jen Osborne's photos are a fantastically enjoyable medley of grinning horses, gold teeth and young love. Her series entitled Llama Love follows an American charity that takes llamas to hospices to cheer people up. The images are simultaneously strange, surreal, uplifting and deftly poignant – the kind of emotional combination beyond many – and Jen is able to tease the viewer with hints of narrative that lead the mind in unexpected directions.

jenosbornestudio.com

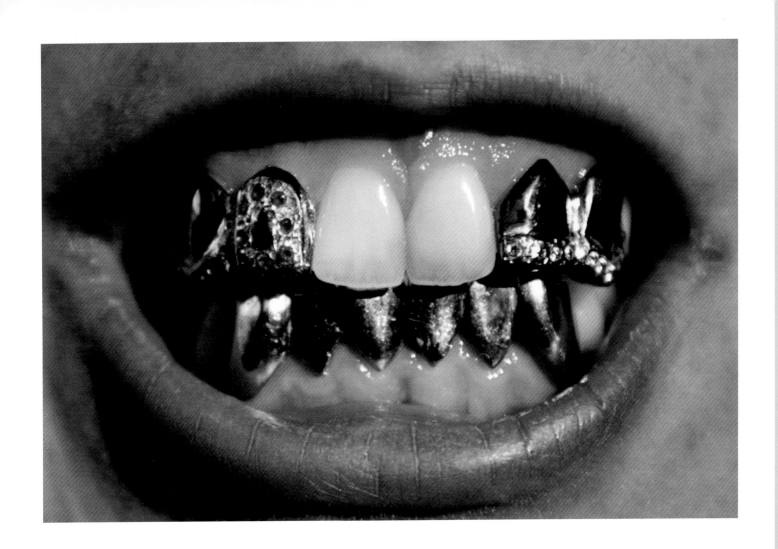

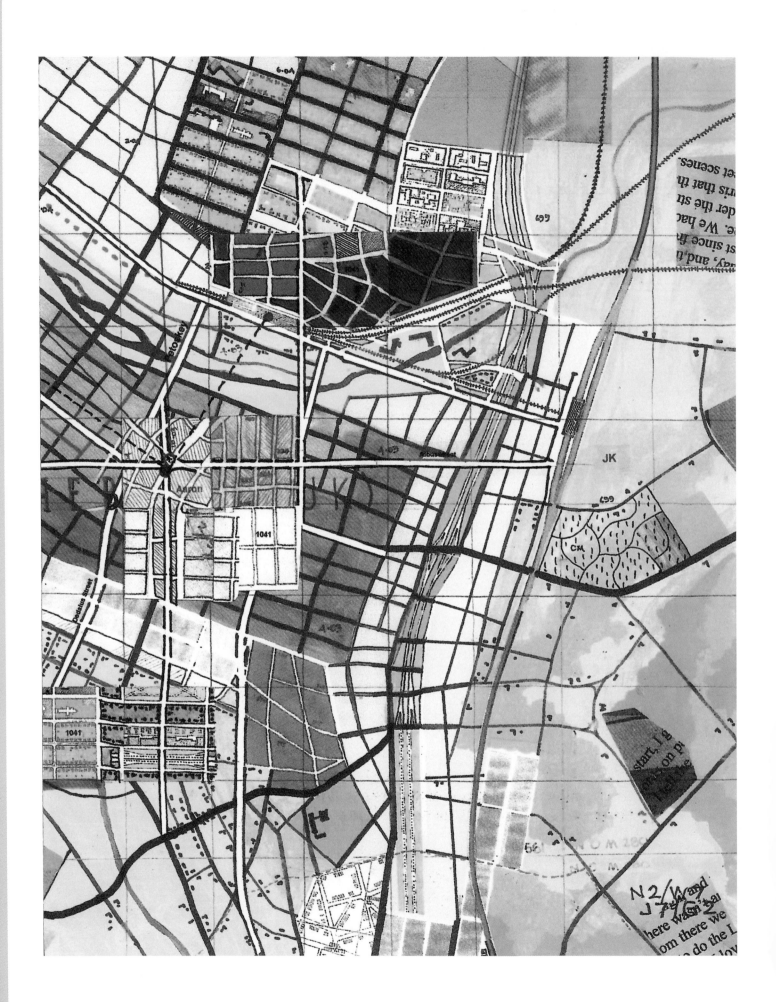

234, 235
Jerry Gretzinger

Over the course of this year 79-year-old Jerry Gretzinger has been celebrated across the world for the persistence of his creative vision. Every day on his coffee break for 30 years, Jerry has worked on one A4 sized section of fictional map at a time, charting a landscape which he creates entirely in his own mind. Safe to say, the idea has grown somewhat since those early days; it now covers 2,500 sheets of paper, and includes train tickets, photographs and magazine cuttings to prevent it from becoming purely representational. What results is an enormous piece of artwork, documenting one man's obsession - and also the man himself.

jerrysmap.blogspot.co.uk

236

Raymond Lemstra

It must be reassuring to be an artist making work that looks entirely unique; it confirms that you've got an original creative mind that's able to produce something all on its own instead of simply referencing other visual material. If you're Raymond Lemstra you've got the added reassurance that the unique work you're producing is really, really good. His frantic illustrations genuinely look like nothing else on earth; the product of an imagination left to wander endlessly and a superior level of draughtsmanship. His laboriously crafted pencil drawings brim with charisma and energy and occupy an anachronistic world that's rich with ancient folklore and the limitless possibilities of an exciting nightmare.

Melange

raymondlemstra.nl

237

Mugi Yamamoto

Printers are a bit like radiators or heart valves in that you only tend to really notice them when they stop working. Anyone who gets too overexcited about them may be considered a bit weird, but not if Mugi Yamamoto has anything to do with it. A recent graduate of the prestigious École Cantonale d'art de Lausanne (ECAL), Mugi's Stack printer loses any form of paper tray and sits instead on top of up to 200 sheets of paper, which it works its way through, stacking the printed pages on top. A brilliant project which spread like wildfire and crowns a super impressive portfolio from a rising design star.

mugiyamamoto.com

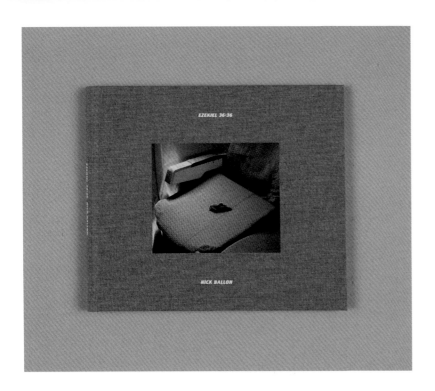

238
Nick Ballon & Studio Thomson

Every year several creatives we've followed for some time produce work which seems to define the start of a new chapter in their career development. Nick Ballon's Ezekiel 36:36 was one such project; a book documenting the world of Bolivian airline Lloyd Aéreo Boliviano; once a great source of national pride but now a run-down, barely surviving symbol of corporate decline. Nick's pictures captured this company and the dedicated people that keep it struggling along with skill and sensitivity and the book itself is the most gorgeous object imaginable with a cloth-bound cover and a terrific insert featuring original graphics from the airline's heyday. A triumph of a publication in every sense.

Editor: Lu Bowman

nickballon.com, studiothomson.com

Peter Mendelsund

We've sung the praises of Peter Mendelsund, art director at Knopf and Pantheon on more than one occasion, both for his remarkable design skills and the way he documents his rigorous process. Peter's the kind of man that likes to have the complete picture before he puts pen to paper and his bibliophile's approach to literature means his book jackets are always incredibly well-informed. Highlights in his concept-driven work include a cover for Nabokov's Lolita that sidesteps cliché, a collection of sketchy covers for Simone De Beauvoir's novels and these beautiful proposals for Julio Cortázar's Hopscotch.

jacketmechanical.blogspot.co.uk

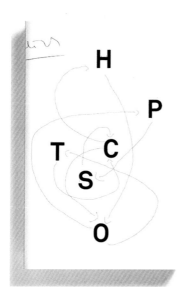
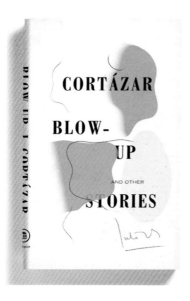

240, 241
Osamu Yokonami

Why did we put Osamu Yokonami in the Annual? Oh, it's because his photos are entirely unique and as visually mesmerising as your favourite Japanese art house film. In this project Osamu took a bunch of girls for a day out in the country to photograph them on the strangest school trips. Wandering into caves, leading each other through snow-covered forests and making spooky formations in green lakes, these images are on the right side of creepy, and we absolutely love them.

yokonamiosamu.jp

242

Pat Bradbury

It's not that we enjoy saying we told you so, but there is a certain amount of satisfaction that comes from finding a young, talented creative that nobody else has heard of and watching them blossom into a beautiful artistic flower. Pat Bradbury is one of our prize orchids in this (torturous) metaphor and we've been taking care of him since he was just a little budding shoot (enough now). Pat was one of our graduates in 2011 and back then we loved him for his witty images and hilarious turns of phrase. Now we still love him for those same reasons, but if it's possible he's become wittier and more talented along the way, which makes us very proud indeed.

Coral Reef

patbradbury.co.uk

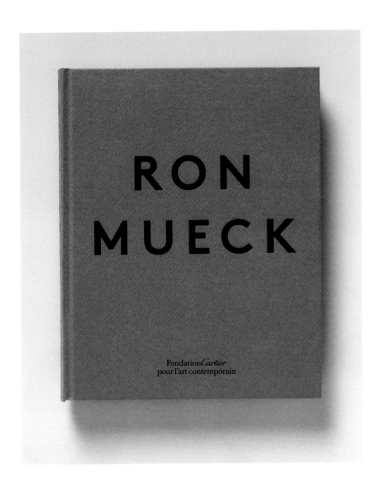

243

Sonya Dyakova

It's wonderful to watch two of the most distinguished creatives working today collaborating on a project, particularly when they operate in such different worlds. In this case the collaboration is a book, but it's a book of Ron Mueck's sculptures designed by Sonya Dyakova. Let's put that into perspective shall we: Ron is one of the world's most renowned artists who shot to fame in 1997 as part of Charles Saatchi's Sensation show. Sonya Dyakova is the art director of frieze magazine, arguably the most respected fine art publication in the world – both major players in their respective fields. Obviously the results are wonderful, and obviously that's why this book had to be included in our own.

atelierdyakova.com

"ge

iconoc

ntly

lastic"

2013

246, 247
Lisa Pacini & Christine Istad

In what may be the most heroic project of the year, Norwegian artists Lisa Pacini and Christine Istad built an enormous LED sun and drove it on a trailer to the parts of the world that get the least daylight hours. The film that accompanies their sometimes treacherous journey reveals a beautiful voyage into some of the most desolate reaches of the earth, and the light that their sun gives off is both metaphorically and literally illuminating. Fingers crossed Lisa and Christine bring their sun back to the UK sometime soon after a flying visit in September.

lisapacini.org, christine-istad.no

248, 249
Olimpia Zagnoli

Illustrator Olimpia Zagnoli slipped unnoticed by us until this summer, when a book of her work tumbled joyfully through our letterbox and had us all gathering around to coo. She has a client list as long as her arm queuing up for her editorial illustration and not without good reason; her instantly recognisable style is centred around witty observations and rendered through vibrant colour and soft shapes to create images which are funny, stylish and discerning in equal measure.

Nostalgia

olimpiazagnoli.com

261
Ana Rita Antonio

A wobbly table leg often encourages the product designer in us all (folded beer mat anyone?) but none to the same extent as Ana Rita Antonio. She came up with 14 inventive ways to replace a table leg; from a stack of books balanced on her head propping it up from underneath, to an intricate system of weights stabilising it from above using materials as eclectic as wellington boots, lamps and potted plants. Brilliant design comes down to creative problem-solving and this is one of the most innovative and unconventional demonstrations of that there skill we've seen all year.

The Poetics of Miss Understanding

cargocollective.com/anaantonio

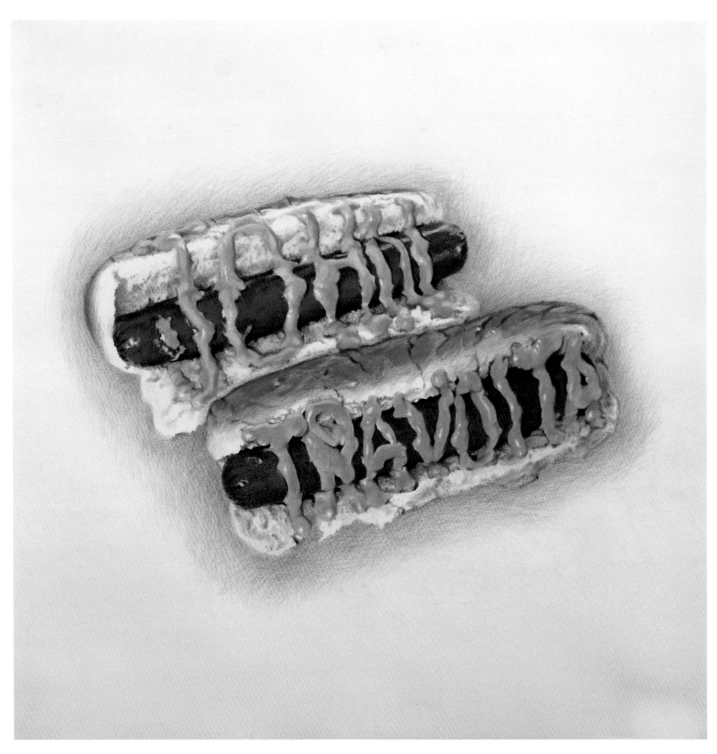

262, 263
Eric Yahnker

When it comes to holding up a mirror to contemporary America, few creatives are able to do it with the same combination of wit and bite as artist Eric Yahnker. The works on display in LA this year included gender swapped superheroes (think Wonder Woman with a hairy chest), Bill Clinton as a sunset and God on the bow of the Titanic in that iconic embrace with Leo. His coruscating critique of a morally-skewed, celebrity-obsessed and culturally confused society resonates all the more because he makes his points with humour and sarcasm rather than one-dimensional tubthumping.

Above: *John Travolta;* Opposite: *Wooly Woman*

ericyahnker.com

264

Colophon

We like Colophon type foundry a heck of a lot; so much so in fact that we've been using their Aperçu face on our website and Annual for the past two years or so. It's not just that they create brilliant fonts that makes them so appealing – that goes without saying – it's also the fact that they produce beautiful specimen books to celebrate every new face they release. This year they announced Archive and popped out a beautiful piece of print to welcome it into the world that shows off the studio's excellent skills both as type designers and print pros. Good work chaps.

colophon-foundry.org